NELSON LANGUAGE ARTS

HAND IN HAND

Cathy Bogusat

Maureen Dockendorf

Barb Eklund

Christine Finochio

Sharon Jeroski

Mary McCarthy

Senior Program Consultant

Jennette MacKenzie

Nelson
Thomson Learning™

Australia • Canada • Denmark • Japan • Mexico • New Zealand • Philippines
Puerto Rico • Singapore • South Africa • Spain • United Kingdom • United States

Grade 3 Reviewers:

Paula Adams
Clarenville, Newfoundland

Susan Bell
Edmonton, Alberta

Brenda Collins
Parkhill, Ontario

Jackie Copp
Winnipeg, Manitoba

Laurel Galt
Whitby, Ontario

Albert Heidt
Regina, Saskatchewan

Betty McWilliam
Lancaster Park, Alberta

Linda Savoy
New Maryland, New Brunswick

Heather Sjoquist
Coquitlam, British Columbia

Jean Voysey
Middleton, Nova Scotia

Corinne Wester
Abbotsford, British Columbia

Equity Consultant:
Ken Ramphal

1120 Birchmount Road
Scarborough, Ontario M1K 5G4
www.nelson.com
www.thomson.com

Printed and bound in Canada
8 9 0 /ITIB/ 8 7 6 5

Canadian Cataloguing in Publication Data

Main entry under title:
Nelson language arts
Contents: [v. 2]. Hand in hand.
ISBN 0-17-618644-1 (v. 2 : bound)
ISBN 0-17-618561-5 (v. 2 : pbk.)
1. Readers (Primary). I. Bogusat, Cathy. II. Title: Nelson
language arts 3.

PE1119.N448 1998   428.6   C98-931518-5

Publisher: Mark Cobham
Executive Editor: Susan Green
Project Editors: Kathleen ffolliott, Norma Kennedy
Art Direction and Production: Liz Harasymczuk
Production Coordinator: Theresa Thomas
Permissions: Karen Taylor

TABLE OF CONTENTS

Unit 2 *Engineer It!* 64

Unit 3 *Good Books, Good Times!* 112

Unit 1: *Hand in Hand*

In this unit, you will read about people and animals who share their lives with one another. As you read about people helping people and animals, sharing knowledge, working together, and just having fun, you will think and talk about similar things that happen to you in your own life. You will

- think and talk about people and animals who are important to you
- learn skills that will help you be a better reader
- compare stories and plays
- use charts, lists, and diagrams to show your ideas
- work with a group to list ways to be a good friend

Mango Morning

Written by Robert Priest
Illustrated by Jenny Campbell

READING TIP

Think about your own life

Think about your friends and what kinds of things
you do together. As you read, compare what the
friends in the poem do together to what you do with
your friends.

We had a mango morning
And everything was sun
We got out on the green grass
And we began to run

And Ishma ran like a river
And Nyima ran like a deer
Eli and I ran like the wind
And now we're standing here

We had an apple noon-time
And everything was sun
We somersaulted softly
And we sang a song for fun

And Ishma sang like a river
And Nyima sang like a sea
And Daniel and I sang Play Play Play
And all was harmony

We had an orange evening
And all the trees were sun
We slid and we were swinging
Till our mothers called us, Come!

And Jemina ran like a river
And Stevie ran like a sea
And Ananda sang like a summer's day
And all was harmony

We had a mango morning
We had an apple noon
We had an orange evening
And then we saw the moon

And Daniel slept like a tiger
And Becky slept like a stream
And Temma slept beside her
And they all began to dream

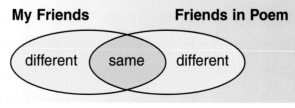

AFTER YOU READ

Make a Venn diagram

Make a Venn diagram showing what is the same and what
is different about friends in your life and the friends
described in the poem.

My Friends   **Friends in Poem**

different   same   different

Stellaluna

Written and illustrated by Janell Cannon

READING TIP

Use pictures to predict

Look at the pictures before you begin to read the story.
They can help you find out who the story is about and
where it takes place. Make a chart like this one and
write down what you think the story will be about.

My Predictions	What Really Happened

In a warm and sultry forest far, far away, there once
lived a mother fruit bat and her new baby.

Oh, how Mother Bat loved her soft tiny baby. "I'll
name you Stellaluna," she crooned.

Each night, Mother Bat would carry Stellaluna
clutched to her breast as she flew out to search for
food.

One night, as Mother Bat followed the heavy scent
of ripe fruit, an owl spied her. On silent wings the
powerful bird swooped down upon the bats.

12

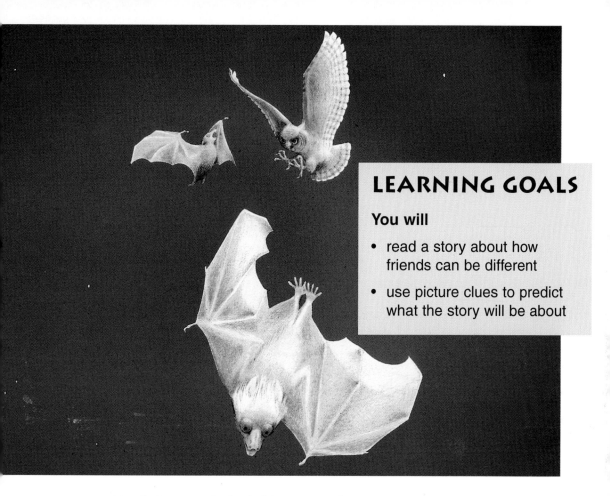

Dodging and shrieking, Mother Bat tried to escape, but the owl struck again and again, knocking Stellaluna into the air. Her baby wings were as limp and useless as wet paper.

Down, down she went, faster and faster, into the forest below.

The dark leafy tangle of branches caught Stellaluna as she fell. One twig was small enough for Stellaluna's tiny feet. Wrapping her wings about her, she clutched the thin branch, trembling with cold and fear.

"Mother," Stellaluna squeaked. "Where are you?"

By daybreak, the baby bat could hold on no longer. Down, down again she dropped.

Flump! Stellaluna landed headfirst in a soft downy nest, startling the three baby birds who lived there.

Stellaluna quickly clambered from the nest and hung out of sight below it. She listened to the babble of the three birds.

"What was *that*?" cried Flap.

"I don't know, but it's hanging by its feet," chirped Flitter.

"Shhh! Here comes Mama," hissed Pip.

Many, many times that day Mama Bird flew away, always returning with food for her babies.

Stellaluna was terribly hungry—but *not* for the crawly things Mama Bird brought.

Finally, though, the little bat could bear it no longer. She climbed into the nest, closed her eyes, and opened her mouth.

Plop! In dropped a big green grasshopper!

Stellaluna learned to be like the birds. She stayed awake all day and slept at night. She ate bugs even though they tasted awful. Her bat ways were quickly disappearing. Except for one thing: Stellaluna still liked to sleep hanging by her feet.

Once, when Mama was away, the curious baby birds decided to try it, too. When Mama Bird came home she saw eight tiny feet gripping the edge of the nest.

"Eeeek!" she cried. "Get back up here this instant! You're going to fall and break your necks!"

The birds clambered back into the nest, but Mama Bird stopped Stellaluna. "You are teaching my children to do bad things. I will not let you back into this nest unless you promise to obey all the rules of this house."

Stellaluna promised. She ate bugs without making faces. She slept in the nest at night. And she didn't hang by her feet. Stellaluna behaved as a good bird should.

All the babies grew quickly. Soon the nest became crowded.

Mama Bird told them it was time to learn to fly. One by one, Pip, Flitter, Flap, and Stellaluna jumped from the nest.

Their wings worked!

I'm just like them, thought Stellaluna. I can fly, too. Pip, Flitter, and Flap landed gracefully on a branch. Stellaluna tried to do the same.

How embarrassing!

I will fly all day, Stellaluna told herself. Then no one will see how clumsy I am.

The next day, Pip, Flitter, Flap, and Stellaluna went flying far from home. They flew for hours, exercising their new wings.

"The sun is setting," warned Flitter.

"We had better go home or we will get lost in the dark," said Flap.

But Stellaluna had flown far ahead and was nowhere to be seen. The three anxious birds went home without her.

All alone, Stellaluna flew and flew until her wings ached and she dropped into a tree. "I promised not to hang by my feet," Stellaluna sighed. So she hung by her thumbs and soon fell asleep.

She didn't hear the soft sound of wings coming near.

"Hey!" a loud voice said. "Why are you hanging upside down?"

Stellaluna's eyes opened wide. She saw a most peculiar face. "I'm not upside down, *you* are!" Stellaluna said.

"Ah, but you're a *bat.* Bats hang by their feet. You are hanging by your thumbs, so that makes you *upside down*!" the creature said. "I'm a bat. I am hanging by my feet. That makes me *right side up*!"

Stellaluna was confused. "Mama Bird told me I was upside down. She said I was wrong...."

"Wrong for a bird, maybe, but not for a bat."

More bats gathered around to see the strange young bat who behaved like a bird. Stellaluna told them her story.

"You ate *b-bugs*?" stuttered one.

"You slept at *night*?" gasped another.

"How very strange," they all murmured.

"Wait! Wait! Let me look at this child." A bat pushed through the crowd. "An *owl* attacked you?" she asked. Sniffing Stellaluna's fur, she whispered, "You are

Stellaluna. You are my baby."

"You escaped the owl?" cried Stellaluna. "You survived?"

"Yes," said Mother Bat as she wrapped her wings around Stellaluna. "Come with me and I'll show you where to find the most delicious fruit. You'll never have to eat another bug as long as you live."

"But it's nighttime," Stellaluna squeaked. "We can't fly in the dark or we will crash into trees."

"We're bats," said Mother Bat. "We can see in darkness. Come with us."

Stellaluna was afraid, but she let go of the tree and dropped into the deep blue sky.

Stellaluna *could* see. She felt as though rays of light shone from her eyes. She was able to see everything in her path.

Soon the bats found a mango tree, and Stellaluna ate as much of the fruit as she could hold.

"I'll never eat another bug as long as I live," cheered Stellaluna as she stuffed herself full. "I must tell Pip, Flitter, and Flap!"

The next day Stellaluna went to visit the birds.

"Come with me and meet my bat family," said Stellaluna.

"Okay, let's go," agreed Pip.

"They hang by their feet and they fly at night and they eat the best food in the world," Stellaluna explained to the birds on the way.

As the birds flew among the bats, Flap said, "I feel upside down here."

So the birds hung by their feet.

"Wait until dark," Stellaluna said excitedly. "We will fly at night."

When night came, Stellaluna flew away. Pip, Flitter, and Flap leaped from the tree to follow her.

"I can't see a thing!" yelled Pip.

"Neither can I," howled Flitter.

"Aaeee!" shrieked Flap.

"They're going to crash," gasped Stellaluna. "I must rescue them!"

Stellaluna swooped about, grabbing her friends in the air. She lifted them to a tree, and the birds grasped a branch. Stellaluna hung from the limb above them.

"We're safe," said Stellaluna. Then she sighed. "I wish you could see in the dark, too."

"We wish you could land on your feet," Flitter replied. Pip and Flap nodded.

They perched in silence for a long time.

"How can we be so different and feel so much alike?" mused Flitter.

"And how can we feel so different and be so much alike?" wondered Pip.

"I think this is quite a mystery," Flap chirped.

"I agree," said Stellaluna. "But we're friends. And that's a fact."

AFTER YOU READ

Check your predictions

Look back at your chart and finish it by writing what really happened in the story. Did the pictures help you to predict what the story would be about?

The Yesterday Stone

Written by Peter Eyvindson
Illustrated by Rhian Brynjolson

READING TIP

Find out how you are like the character

Think about the people in your life who believe in you.
How do you know they believe in you? Read to see
how Anna began to believe in her friend.

Others didn't believe Anna when she told them how she liked to get up early to run outside and hear the bees in the meadow making their new morning song. A special song meant only for Anna.

But Molly believed.

And when Anna told them all to smile at dandelions, and watch them smile back, they laughed at her. But not Molly.

LEARNING GOALS

You will

- read a story about friends who believe in each other

- put yourself in the character's place

Molly didn't laugh. She spent the whole afternoon smiling down at dandelions. Every last dandelion. And when she was finished, Molly said it was true. Dandelions did make her happy.

But Anna didn't know if she should show her the yesterday stone. Would Molly believe?

Her grandmother, the one who taught her about bee songs and dandelions, had given her the yesterday stone. And it was her grandmother who had warned her.

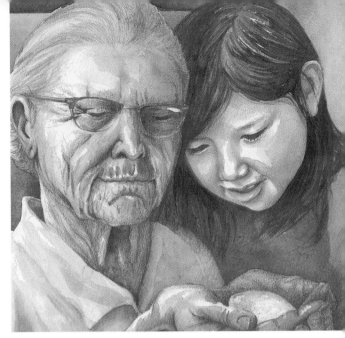

"Be careful," she said. "There are those who will not believe in the yesterday stone."

She remembered how grandmother rolled the polished stone between her soft and wrinkled fingers. Roll and polish. Polish and roll. Roll and polish.

She would rub the stone over and over before she would pause for a moment, open her hands like a cup, and peer in. Again she would close her hands and again she would rub the stone.

"The yesterday stone needs warmth before we begin," she would say while she rolled and polished the stone.

"Ah, there," she sighed as she cupped her hands close to her face to see. "There it is. The yesterday stone is ready."

Anna would climb up beside her grandmother and pull the gentle hands down just enough so that she too could have a look.

The yesterday stone always glowed like morning sunlight pouring through a window. And looking through that tiny window cupped inside her grandmother's hands, Anna would see a different world.

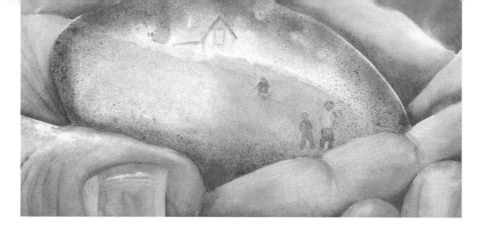

Sometimes it would be a world of shining knights and fairy princesses, or sometimes a world of pirates, villains, and rogues. Those were exciting worlds.

But the world that Anna liked best was Grandmother's world, the world when Grandmother was young.

"There!" Grandmother would say. "Do you see him? The tall one with the rubber boots? That's your Great Uncle Vernon. And the little one? He's Uncle Roy. And see the little girl? That's me. When I was called Mary. In the springtime, when we couldn't take the buggy to school, Vernon always got to wear those boots.

"Look! See how we're coming to a puddle? Watch to see what happens."

Anna would pull her grandmother's hand a little closer and watch as the tiny figures came to the puddle. Vernon would wade across first. He'd stop on the far side, pull off the rubber boots, and toss them back across the puddle. Next, Roy would pull on the boots and wade across. When he had completed the journey, the boots were tossed back for Mary to use.

"We had only one pair of boots among the three of us, because Mother and Father couldn't afford any others. I'll never forget how big those boots felt."

"Grandmother," asked Anna, "could I keep your yesterday stone?"

"No!" said Grandmother. "No!" Abruptly, her hands closed to shut out that other world. "No. You mustn't have it. It is my yesterday stone."

Anna was puzzled. "Grandmother, why? What's the matter?"

For a long moment, Grandmother was silent before she turned to look carefully into Anna's eyes.

"Anna," she said. "You cannot have my yesterday stone. You must find your own."

"How can I do that, Grandmother?" Anna asked. "Where can I find one?"

Grandmother cupped her hands and whispered to her yesterday stone. "Is it time?"

"Yes!" Grandmother smiled. "It is time. But we must be careful."

She got up, went swiftly to her desk drawer, and pulled out a magnet tied to a long string.

"Come along, my dear. We must find your yesterday stone."

Anna ran eagerly along behind while Grandmother strode out the front door, down the steps, and out to the gravel road.

"I want you to know, Anna, that you must always believe. There are those who will believe in your yesterday stone and there are those who will not. Be careful of those who do not, for they are the ones who will convince you not to believe.

"Do you understand?"

"Yes," whispered Anna.

"Good. Let us begin. Here, you must hold the string."

Grandmother bent over and carefully laid the magnet on the ground.

"Pull, Anna. But be gentle."

The magnet bumped over the stones as Anna began to tug.

"No! No! Anna. Be gentle. Ever so gentle. Your yesterday stone needs time to speak."

Grandmother took hold of her hand and with the string slowly, ever so slowly, pulled the magnet along.

"There, now. Try again."

Grandmother let go, allowing Anna to pull the string on her own. Anna watched every stone carefully. She hoped it would be pretty. Like the spotted one. The one that looked like a sparrow's egg.

"Is that it?" she asked Grandmother.

"No. No, Anna," chuckled Grandmother. "If you must ask, then it cannot be the one. You will know, Anna. You will know when your yesterday stone speaks."

Patiently, Anna pulled the magnet up the road waiting, listening, wanting every stone to speak. But she heard nothing, saw nothing, felt nothing. Until ... until she felt it ... a warm tingle. Anna knew. It was the one. Her yesterday stone had spoken.

Grandmother bent over quickly and carefully picked the stone up. "Here you are, my dear. Here is your yesterday stone."

It was an ordinary looking stone but Anna could rub and polish, polish and rub, rub and polish her way into other worlds, those exciting worlds of knights and pirates, those worlds her grandmother had shown her. But what Anna found most exciting was her yesterday stone gave her some worlds of her own.

Anna always knew the stone was there—tucked away in the bottom of her pocket underneath bits of string, a few marbles, a yo-yo, and a magnet.

She knew it was there but just to be certain she secretly slipped her hand inside her pocket to finger the crisp red paper wrapped carefully around her yesterday stone.

It was there all right. But still she didn't know if she should show it to Molly.

Would Molly believe?

"There are those who will believe in your yesterday stone," Grandmother had said, "and there are those who will not."

For a long moment, Anna silently stared into the distance before she looked carefully into Molly's eyes.

"Molly believes in dandelions," whispered Anna. "Will she believe in you?"

Anna waited for the answer.

"Yes," whispered Anna. "Molly will believe."

"Molly," she said as she pulled her hand from her pocket and began to unwrap the red tissue. "I have something to show you."

AFTER YOU READ

Make a list

Describe what makes a friend someone you can believe in. What words would you use to describe a friend?

My Buddy

Written by Audrey Osofsky
Illustrated by Ted Rand

Buddy is my best friend. He never gets mad at me. He never runs off to play with another boy. He always listens when I need someone to talk to.

Buddy is my golden retriever. He looks like the sun is always shining on him. When he sees me, his big brown eyes are sweet as a smile.

But Buddy is more than my friend. He's my arms and legs. He helps me do things I can't do by myself.

And I can't do a lot of things other kids can. I have a disease that makes my muscles weak. It's called 'muscular 'dystrophy. 营养失调

Before Buddy, Mom and Dad helped me. Mike and other friends helped too. But friends sometimes get tired of helping. And I wanted to do things on my own.

Buddy was my wish come true. We met at a camp where Buddy was trained to help someone like me.

As a puppy, he was special. Loving and smart, he was chosen to be a Service Dog. Buddy was the star of puppy kindergarten. Top dog in his graduation class. In two years, Buddy had learned sixty commands.

I had to learn all the commands in two weeks. I had to learn how to take care of Buddy, too.

It was hard. Much harder than I thought. We worked long hours and had tests every day.

Over and over I practised giving commands. It wasn't easy to make Buddy obey me. He acted like a kid who didn't pay any attention to his teacher.

Many times I'd get angry. Sometimes I cried. But I never gave up, even when I wanted to. I wanted Buddy more.

To help us bond, to feel that we belonged together, Buddy was leashed to my wrist all day and night. We had to do everything together. We slept together. We even took showers together!

I began to understand
Buddy better. And myself,
too. I had to believe I was
a leader before Buddy would
believe. After many days, my voice got stronger
when I gave commands.

One day Buddy looked me in the eye—and obeyed.
He learned to trust me, and I learned to trust him.

Then I graduated too, and we were a team.

Back home, Mike came over to meet my new
friend.

"Don't pet him or give him snacks," I said. "Buddy
doesn't eat on the job."

I told Mike about the sixty commands, but I just
showed him a few.

"Up, light!" I commanded, and Buddy turned on
the light. "Good boy!"

"Tug!" I commanded, and Buddy opened our front
door.

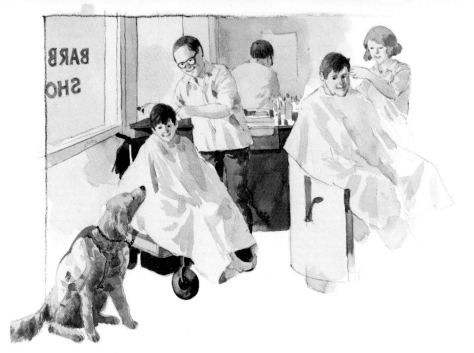

"Let me try!" Mike said.

"Buddy only listens to me," I told him.

"You're lucky," Mike said.

We went to the shopping mall. I worried. Would Buddy keep his cool in a crowd?

Buddy was a pro. He pushed elevator buttons, fetched baseball cards from a high shelf, and kept me 理发匠 company at the barbershop.

Buddy's favourite job was at the pet store. He picked up a bag of doggy treats, gave the lady my dollar, and brought me the package with the change inside, wagging his tail.

On the first day of school, Buddy brought me my
clothes. Then he fetched his blue-and-gold backpack.
He was ready to work.   来率

Mom zipped up my lunch, notebook, and pencils
in Buddy's pack and <u>clipped</u> it on his back. She gave
me a hug. She wanted to give Buddy a hug too, but she
couldn't, because he was working.

We rode to school together on our special bus. I
wondered if kids would think it was weird to see a boy
in a wheelchair with a dog in school. Maybe the
teacher wouldn't want a dog in her class. Kids might
play with him and he'd bark and act goofy.

At first, everyone wanted to pet Buddy.

"Buddy is a working dog, not a pet," the teacher
explained. "His sign says 'Don't Touch' so he can keep
his mind focused on his work."

focus attention on

Buddy fetched a pencil I had dropped, and kids said he was handy. Buddy brought me a book from the library shelf, and they said he was smart. In the lunchroom, Buddy retrieved my empty milk carton from the trash can, and they laughed and said he was funny.

Now the kids are used to a dog in school. When Buddy takes a nap, they step over him. He's just one of the guys.

My teacher likes Buddy too. He's the quietest one in the class.

After school, Buddy is ready for a run around our yard. On nice days, we play ball outside. I can't throw the ball very far, but Buddy doesn't care. He's just happy to play with me.

Sometimes Mike calls. Buddy picks up the phone and brings it to me.

"Excuse me, (but) this is my floor"

"Come on over and play video games," Mike says.

We buzz over to Mike's house. Buddy rings the doorbell.

Buddy likes playing T Ball the best. I hit the Wiffle ball with a plastic bat and Buddy does the fielding. Whatever we do, we do together. We're a team.

Before Buddy, I didn't like to go places. People stared at me. Now people look at *us*—and ask about my dog.

Buddy is my best friend, I tell them.

At bedtime, I brush his shiny coat. Soon I'm tired and have to stop. Buddy licks my face. He knows I'm his best friend too.

"Up, switch!" I command, and Buddy turns off the light.

He gives me sloppy kisses. I give him hugs back. He's my Buddy.

AFTER YOU READ

Find answers

Look back at the questions you had about dogs like Buddy. Were there any questions the story didn't answer? Where would be a good place to find answers to those questions?

Stone Soup

Written by Jeff Siamon

READING TIP

Note features of a play

The form of a play is different from a story. It shows what different characters say and do. As you read, think about how those features help you read.

List of Players

- Narrator
- Jan
- Jan's Brother
- Jan's Mother
- Jan's Father
- The People of Lost Lake

The Narrator is standing at one side of the stage. Behind the Narrator is a sign that reads: Stone Soup. Get your amazing stones. Only $1. *In the front and centre of the stage is a large pot. At the other side of the stage is Jan's family car. In the background are the houses of Lost Lake.*

STONE SOUP

Get your Amazing Stones
ONLY $1!

Narrator: Stone soup! Stone soup! Step right up boys and girls. Get your A-MAZ-ING stones for stone soup. Only *one* loonie! That's right. Only *one* loonie buys you a chance to make stone soup.... What's that? *Never* heard of stone soup? Why it's the most A-MAZ-ING soup in the world! It will fill you up. Bring tears to your eyes. Make your tummy purr. And you only need *one* thing to make it. This A-MAZ-ING, EX-TRA-OR-DIN-ARY, FAN-TAS-TIC stone! *(kisses stone)*

What's that? You don't believe me? Impossible!
Why *everybody's* heard of stone soup. Put up your
hands if you've ever heard of stone soup. *(looks at
audience)* Hmmm.... Put up your hands if you've
ever heard of *wood* soup.... Hmmm. Put up your
hands if you've ever heard of *mud* soup....
Hmmm. Put up your hands if you've ever *put up
your hands*. Aha! *(The Narrator looks around at the
audience.)* Well, let me tell you the *real* story of
stone soup. You can decide if it's true or not.
(walks over to pot) One day, Jan and her family
went for a drive in the country.

Jan's family enters and sits in car.

Brother: I'm hungry. I want a drink of water.

Jan: Just where are we going, Dad?

Father: Uh.... *(Father and Mother look at each other.)*

Narrator: Jan's parents looked at each other and realized they were lost.

Mother: I think we're lost.

Jan: Lost!

Brother: Just where is Lost?

Narrator: Now that was a good question because just at that moment ... *(A loud crash is heard. Jan's family falls out of car.)* ... the car hit a rock and everyone tumbled out onto the ground.

Person #1 walks across stage holding a sign. It reads: "Lost Lake. Population 65 ... and falling."

Jan: Did you see a sign back there?

Father: No, where? *(Person #1 walks back across stage holding sign.)*

Jan: That sign.

Mother: *(not paying attention)* What sign? *(Person #1 walks back across stage with sign.)*

Brother: That sign!

Father and Mother: *(still not paying attention)* We didn't see any sign. *(Person #1 walks up to Mother and Father and shows them the sign.)*

Person 1: This sign!

Father: Oh.

Mother: *(reading sign)* Lost Lake. Population 65 ... and falling. *(Person #1 exits.)*

Jan: Where's Lost Lake? *(Everyone shrugs.)*

Narrator: Now Lost Lake is in the middle of Nowhere. Just on the other side of Somewhere. And around the corner from Anywhere. So it's not surprising they had never heard of it.

Brother: I'm hungry.

Jan: Me, too.

Narrator: *(walks back to side of stage)* Jan's family set out to find the town. Now they were all hungry. And they needed to get their car fixed.

Jan's family goes up to House #1.

Mother: *(knocks on door)* Hello.
Person 2: *(behind House #1)* Go away. We're not home.
Father: But we're hungry. Our children are hungry.
Mother: And we need to fix our car.
Person 3: *(behind House #1)* Go away.
Person 4: *(behind House #1)* We're not home.

Family goes to House #2.

Father: *(knocks on door)* Anybody home?
Person 5: *(behind House #2)* We're not home.
Person 6: *(behind House #2)* Go away.
Narrator: No one in the town wanted to help Jan's family. You see, the people of Lost Lake had no money and very little food. They didn't want to give these strangers any help.
Person 9: *(behind House #4)* Go away. We can't help you.
Person 5: *(behind House #2)* Go away.
Narrator: See?

Jan goes to House #4. The rest of the family follows.

All: We're not home! Go away! We're not home! Go away!

Narrator: Poor Jan and her family. The people of Lost Lake were afraid of strangers. And they never shared their food. Not even among themselves.

Person 8: We never share our food. Not with anyone.

Narrator: Just then Jan had an idea. A RE-MARK-ABLE idea.

Jan: I know what we can do. We don't need their food. We can make stone soup.

Father: *(thinking)* Hmmm. Stone soup.

Jan: That's right. And it will taste better than any food they can give.

Person 4: *(behind House #2)* Stone soup? *(comes out of house)*

Person 8: *(behind House #3)* Stone soup? *(comes out of house)*

Person 10: *(behind House #4)* What's stone soup? *(comes out of house)*

Jan: What's stone soup?!

Narrator: Why it's the most EX-TRA-OR-DIN-ARY, the most FAN-TAS-TIC ...

Jan: ... soup in the world. That's all. *(All the Townspeople come out of their houses.)*

Person 3: Stone soup?

Person 7: Made from stones?

Person 2: And it tastes good?

Jan: The best soup in the world.

Brother: Better than pizza.

Person 1: *(goes to Jan)* Please, miss. How do you make stone soup?

All: Yes. How do you make stone soup?

Mother: Oh, they don't need stone soup. They have lots of food to eat.

Person 4: No we don't. Please tell us.

Person 6: We'll even help you make it.

All: Please tell us.

Jan: Well ... first we need a big pot.

Person 2: *(goes to pot)* Here is a pot.

Father: And we'll need water to fill the pot.

Brother: And wood to make a fire.

Person 7: Here is the water. *(pours water into pot)*

Person 3: And here is some wood. *(puts wood around pot)*

Jan: Next we need three very special stones.

Person 1: That's easy. All we have are stones.

Person 10: Too many stones.

Person 5: *(brings three stones and a large spoon)* Here.

Jan: Thank you. *(puts stones into pot, stirs, and takes a sip)* Hmmm. It's good, but....

Person 5: But what?

Jan: But you know, salt and pepper would make it taste even better.

Person 2: That's a good idea. I'll get the salt and pepper. *(gets salt and pepper and puts it into soup)*

Mother: *(tastes soup)* Hmmm. It's good, but....

Person 7: But what?

Mother: But I bet if it had some carrots, it would taste even better.

Person 4: Carrots! What a great idea! I'll get you some carrots. *(adds carrots to soup)*

Brother: *(tastes soup)* Hmmm.

Jan: *(tastes soup)* Hmmm. It tastes good, but....

All: But what?

Jan: But if we only had some potatoes.

Father: Potatoes would make it taste even better.

Person 9: I have some potatoes. *(puts potatoes into soup)*

Jan stirs and carefully tastes soup. Everyone watches.

Jan: It's good, but....

All: BUT WHAT?

Jan: But there's still something missing. Maybe it's the cabbage.

Person 4: I have two cabbages. *(puts cabbages into soup)*

Jan: Or maybe it's onions.

Person 1: Didn't you put any onions in?

Father: No. I guess we forgot.

Person 10: How can you make soup without onions? I have some onions. Why didn't you ask? *(puts in onions)*

Father: *(sips soup)* Good ... but....

All: BUT WHAT?

Father: *(to Person #3)* Here, you taste. Don't you think it needs a little celery?

Person 3: *(tastes soup)* Definitely.

Person 2: I have some celery. *(puts in celery)*

Mother: And maybe if it had some turnips.

Jan: And some beef bones.

Brother: And some rice.

Father: And some beef, too.

Person 5: I have some turnips.

Person 7: I have some beef.

Person 2: I have some rice.

Person 10: And I'll put in a whole box of tomatoes.

Everyone puts food in. Jan stirs and tastes soup.

All: How is it now?

Jan: PERFECT!

Person 8: Well everyone, let's eat!

Person 1: I'll bring the bowls and spoons.

Person 5: I'll bring some bread.

Person 2: Why don't we go to my house? We can set up tables in the backyard.

Jan: What a good idea.

(Everyone but the Narrator starts to exit.)

Person 9: I have three chickens that I can bring.

Person 6: And I'll make a salad.

Jan: Great!

All: Let's have a party!

(*Everyone exits.*)

Narrator: (*goes to pot*) Well, that's what they did. They had a party. A great party. With bread and cheese and chickens and steaks and salad and juice and ... of course, STONE SOUP. And everyone said it was the best soup they had ever had. And the best party. *Now,* put up your hands if you've ever heard of stone soup.

AFTER YOU READ

Make a chart

Look back at the play and make a chart of the text features of the play.

Feature	Example

Red Bird

Written by Barbara Mitchell
Illustrated by Todd L. W. Doney

READING TIP

Make mind pictures

Authors make pictures with words. As you
read, use the author's words to make pictures
in your mind.

Mom takes the regalia out of the trunk. Doeskin
dresses, buckskin leggings, soft beaded
moccasins, Katie's scarlet shawl. It's
September, time for the Nanticoke powwow.
Dad loads the camper with cooking pots and
blankets, drumsticks, rattles, and jingling bells. He
places his feather headdress proudly on top of it all.

53

Off to the powwow they go. Away from the screaming sirens and honking horns. Away from crowded buildings that scrape the city sky. Down past Dover Air Force Base, where jets roar over the camper like giant claps of thunder.

Suddenly they are in the country. Fields stretch flat and green as far as Katie can see. LIVE CRABS—HARD AND SOFT, roadside signs cry out.

"We're almost there," says Dad. He rolls down his window to breathe in bayside air.

"Long before the European settlers came, Nanticoke held the crab feasts. They fished the Delaware Bay."

美国新泽西州和特拉华州之间的西洋海湾

Around by Nanticoke cornfields golden in the sun, the world is strangely quiet. There is nothing to be heard. Nothing but summer crickets chirping their goodbyes. And from the distant pine trees, the beating of Nanticoke drums.

Down the sandy roadside, the drums call Katie's name: Red Bird, Red Bird, RED BIRD, RED BIRD. "Katie" fades away. She is Red Bird, Nanticoke Daughter. She hears her people singing. She hears the calling drums: Hurry, Red Bird, hurry! The powwow has begun.

Dad parks the camper deep in the fragrant pines. Grandma and Grandpa are there. And aunts and uncles and cousins, all the way from Canada. Grandpa scoops Red Bird into his arms. "Red Bird, you've come!"

Over in the arena, the Nanticoke chief takes his place. "The drumbeat is our heartbeat," Chief Red Deer says. He calls for all the dancers. "Nanticoke ... Delaware ... Rose Bud Sioux. Cherokee ... Iroquois." The dancers enter from the east, like the rising sun.

Red Bird moves into the circle. Step-STEP, step-STEP. Step-STEP, step-STEP. The singing grows louder. The drumbeat grows stronger. Red Bird's heart beats with joy.

Dancing makes Red Bird hungry. Fry bread puffs and sizzles. "Honey on mine," says Mom. Dad smears his with butter. Red Bird chooses spicy beans.

Under rainbow-coloured tents, traders show their wares. A Cherokee necklace? An Iroquois rattle, a turtle carved of bone? What shall Red Bird buy?

At last she decides. She must have the headband with *Nanticoke* spelled out in tiny beads.

"Shawl dancers, take your places," Chief Red Deer calls.

Dipping, gliding, turning, fluttering her shawl like wings—she *is* Red Bird, wonderful creature, beautiful bird of the earth.

At night around the campfire, Grandpa tells his tales. Stories of Turtle Island—the earth—and how it came to be. "Walk softly on Mother Earth," he says.

The fire burns low. Mom and Dad go off to sleep in the camper. Red Bird and her cousins sleep with Grandma and Grandpa in the tent. Snug in Nanticoke blankets, they dream their Nanticoke dreams.

In the morning, the dancing and feasting begin again. Red Bird wishes the powwow could go on forever.

But all too soon it is time to pack up and go home. Red Deer calls for the final dance. "We dance the Round Dance—the dance of all peoples," the chief explains to the spectators. "Come, take hands and join in."

Red feet and white feet, black feet and yellow feet step to the beat of the heart. Then the dancers slip out to the west, like the setting sun. The drumbeat grows softer and softer: RED BIRD, RED BIRD, Red Bird, Red Bird. "Red Bird" fades away.

On Monday, Mom puts on her uniform and goes to her work at the hospital. Dad returns to his office. Katie is off to school. The regalia is back in the attic.

The beaded Nanticoke headband stays in Katie's dresser drawer. On moon-bright nights in winter, Katie will take it out and sit by her window and look into the city sky. She will hear her people singing. She will hear the far-off drums. The heartbeat of The People stays with her all year long.

AFTER YOU READ

Use describing words

Draw one of the mind pictures you saw as you read the describing words in the story. Around the picture, write the describing words the author used.

Hand in Hand

In this unit, you read about friends who play together and work together. Now it is your turn to work in a group and make a list of things you need to do to be a good friend.

⋯▶ Before You Begin

Think about working in a group.
- How will the group work together?
- What do we need to talk about before we start ?
- What do I think makes a good friend?

Group Members ...
- take turns
- listen to each other
- ask questions
- stay on topic
- include everyone
- respect all ideas
- work together

Here are Kelly's notes about what makes a good friend.

A good friend is someone who
- shares with me
- I like
- listens and talks to me
- likes me
- cares about me
- is honest
- is trusting
- helps me

Your First Draft

1 **Brainstorm ideas about what good friends do.**

- Choose someone in the group to take notes.
- Take turns telling what being a friend means.
- Include everyone's ideas.

2 **Decide how many points to include on your list.**

- Discuss each idea to decide whether it should be included.
- Circle the points you want to keep.

3 **Talk about how you will present your ideas.**

Remember, when you work together:

- Cooperate!
- Contribute!
- Celebrate!

Here is part of the list Kelly's group made. They marked the points about being a friend that they wanted to present.

Qualities we Look for in A Good Friend

- (Someone who Shares)
- (Someone who is nice)
- someone who we get along well with
- someone who keeps promises
- someone who asks you what you want to do
- someone who has a good personality

61

Revise and Edit

- Post your list of ideas about what makes a good friend where everyone in the group can see it.
- Read the list together. Do any points seem more important than others?
- Put the points in order.
- Correct the spelling, grammar, and punctuation in the points you want to present.

Choose five ideas from your group list. A short list will be easier for people to read *and* remember.

Here is the list of points Kelly's group chose to present.

GOod Friends Are...

Someone who shares

Someone who is nice

Someone who takes turns

Someone who helps you

Someone who is honest

Publish It

Your ideas about what makes a good friend can be displayed in many ways. You can:

- Make a poster.
- Put your list in your school or class newsletter.
- Post a different idea each week in different places in your classroom.
- Make a booklet and draw a picture to go with each idea.

Think About Your Learning

Did we:

- Listen to each other?
- Take turns?
- Share jobs while we worked?
- Encourage each other?
- Present our ideas neatly?

Unit 2: *Engineer It!*

In this unit, you will find out about shapes and building—which shapes are best for building and why, how to make model structures, and how to test structures. You will

- read articles, diagrams, and pictures to get information
- follow and give directions
- look for ways that writers make instructions easy to follow
- list words and terms that are special to structures and shapes
- build your own cardboard structure

UGG
GIBBONS

▲ ● ■ ▼ ◆ ▲ ● ■ ▼ ◆

Shapes All Around Us

▲ ● ■ ▼ ◆ ▲ ● ■ ▼ ◆

Written by Susan Green

Take a look around you. The world is full of shapes. In the country or in the city, at home or in your neighbourhood, shapes are everywhere. No one would be able to build or make things without them.

The next time you go for a walk or a drive, see how many shapes you can find. Look for different ways that shapes are used. You'll be amazed at how many shapes you discover in the world around you.

There are shapes where you play.

There are shapes where you live.

Nature's builders use shapes, too.
Look around. What shapes do you see?

The Terrific Triangle

Written by Susan Hughes

READING TIP

Use picture cues

As you read about the triangle, look at the pictures. Use the pictures to help you understand the information.

Shapes are part of the solid world around you. You can see shapes in living things, like flowers and leaves. You can also see shapes in the things that have been made by people. When people make things, they often begin by using a simple shape, like a circle, a square, or a triangle. How do they decide what shape to use? It depends on what they are making and what it will be used for.

压扁

Say that they are going to make a structure, such as a bridge, or a vehicle, such as a bicycle. Bridges and bicycles carry things, such as cars and people. They need to remain stiff and strong, so they won't be <u>squashed</u> out of shape by the things they are carrying. Different shapes are stronger than others. The triangle is the strongest shape of all! That's why it is used in making things from bridges to bicycles.

A pyramid has sides in the shape of a triangle. They meet in a point at the top. Their triangular shape has helped pyramids last for over 3000 years.

A wedge also has sides in the shape of a triangle. This tapering shape is very strong. Wedges can be used to do the hard work of holding doors open or prying things apart.

dʒi əʊ e sɪk

A geodesic dome is made up of many triangles. Look at how the dome in this playground is strong enough to hold these children on it!

Look around you. See how many things you can find that are made using the most stable shape of all: the terrific triangle!

1. Bend a plastic straw into the shape of a square.

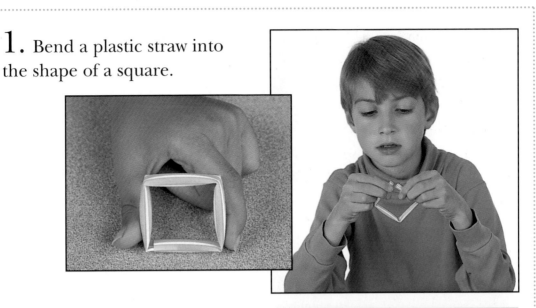

2. Push gently on one of the corners of the straw square. The lengths of the square's sides don't change. But look— see how two of the square's *angles* get bigger and two of the square's angles get smaller? The square can easily change into a diamond shape.

This means it isn't a very stable shape. It wouldn't be used to make a bridge or a bicycle. A bridge or bicycle that easily changes shape would spell disaster!

3. Now bend a plastic straw into the shape of a triangle. The triangle has only three sides.

Push gently on one of the corners. This doesn't change the lengths of the triangle's sides, so the angles don't change either. The sides remain stiff. The triangle is a very stable shape.

AFTER YOU READ

Think about your learning

Look back at the pictures. How did they help you understand the information?

The Eiffel Tower

Written by Etta Kaner
Illustrated by Pat Cupples

READING TIP

Think about what you know

Think about what you already know about structures.
Sketch how you would build a tall tower to keep it from
blowing over. Read to see what one builder did.

When Alexandre Gustave Eiffel designed his now-famous tower, many people called it the "awful" tower instead of the Eiffel tower. Well-known composers, artists, and writers signed a form asking the French government not to build the tower. But the government wanted to have an unusual tower that would attract visitors to the 1889 Paris World's Fair. So, on January 26, 1887, construction began on what became the world's tallest tower at that time.

Eiffel's main challenge was to make sure that strong winds would not topple his 300-m tower. He solved this problem in several ways. He built a strong base, or *foundation*, for each of the four "legs" that supported the tower. He also set the "legs" far enough apart (one and a quarter football fields) to support such a great height. And, strange as it may seem,

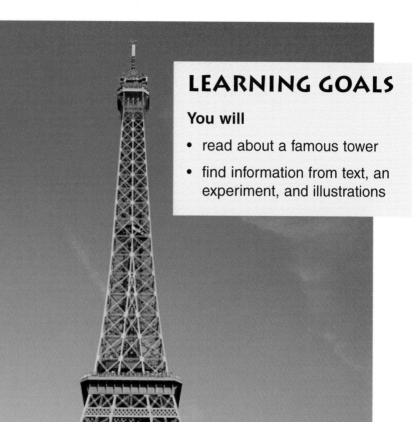

LEARNING GOALS

You will

- read about a famous tower
- find information from text, an experiment, and illustrations

he used the spaces between the steel beams of the tower to strengthen it. How is this possible?

Try this experiment to find out.

You will need:

- 2 large empty cereal boxes the same size
- scissors
- an electric fan

1. Close the lid of one box and set it aside.

2. Cut four large triangles out of the front of the second box so that an X frame is left, as shown.

3. Do the same to the back of the box.

4. Close the lid of the box.

5. One at a time, stand each box 1 m away from the fan. What do you think will happen when you turn on the fan?

6. Turn on the fan and watch each box for one minute. What happens? Why?

What's Going On?

The box with the open spaces allows some wind to go through the spaces rather than push against the box. That's why the box does not fall over. The box without the spaces has more surface for the wind to push against, and so it eventually falls over.

The Eiffel Tower is built out of steel triangles that let the wind blow through instead of pushing against it.

AFTER YOU READ

Think about what you have learned

Think about what you learned about structures from the text, experiment, and illustrations. Use what you learned to make changes to your sketch.

Skyscrapers

Written by Etta Kaner
Illustrated by Pat Cupples

Just like your skeleton gives your body its shape, a framework of steel (or sometimes concrete) columns and beams gives a skyscraper its shape. *Columns* are posts that are attached vertically (up and down) to each other to give the skyscraper its height. *Beams* reach horizontally (across) from one column to another to form a box-like framework with the columns. When you look at a steel column or beam from its end, each one is shaped like a capital letter "I" for strength. What makes this shape so strong? Make some "I" columns and find out.

column

beam

LEARNING GOALS

You will

- read about how the structure of skyscrapers gives them their strength

- use graphics to find information

Make some "I" columns.

You will need:

- 2 sheets of construction paper, each 23 cm x 30 cm
- scissors
- a ruler
- a pencil
- glue

1. Cut two strips of paper, each 5 cm x 23 cm.

3. Fold the edges of the paper up along the two drawn lines.

2. On one strip, draw two lines 1.25 cm in from each long edge.

4. Mark and fold the other strip the same way.

5. Glue the two strips back to back to make an "I" column.

7. Glue a strip on each outer side of one of the "I" columns.

6. Make another column the same way. Then cut two strips of paper, each 2.5 cm x 23 cm.

8. Stand the two columns upright. Press down on each column. Which one buckles first?

What's Going On?

Are you surprised at how strong the paper columns are? The "I" column doesn't <u>buckle</u> easily because most of the paper is spread out away from its centre line. The more the material is spread out from the centre line, the stronger a column is. That is why the column was even stronger when you added the two outer strips. Steel columns used for building skyscrapers are strong because of their "I" shape and the strength of steel.

The beams that join the columns are also "I"-shaped but are deeper than columns. They look more like this. Beams are attached to columns with bolts or by welding (melting the metal connection points together).

Build Your Own Skyscraper

Why not construct your own skyscraper? Use "I" columns and beams like the ones you just made. Make a framework as tall and as wide as you want. Instead of digging a foundation, tape the bottom columns to a sheet of cardboard to support your skyscraper. Attach the beams to the columns with tape. Each column will be tall enough to support two storeys. Once you have built your framework, lay cardboard floors on the beams and glue paper to the frame for the outside walls.

Swaying in the Wind

If you were on the top floor of a very tall skyscraper on a windy day, you might feel a little sick. That's because the building is swaying back and forth. This swaying is called *wind drift*. In a building as tall as the 72-storey First Canadian Place in Toronto, Ontario, the wind drift can be up to one metre in each direction.

To limit the amount of wind drift in a skyscraper, engineers sometimes put a giant concrete block weighing a few hundred tonnes on the roof. This block is called a *tuned mass damper*. Springs on two sides of the damper attach it to the walls of the roof. The damper is specially designed so that when a strong wind pushes the skyscraper in one direction, the damper slides in the opposite direction. The great weight of the block prevents the building from swaying too much.

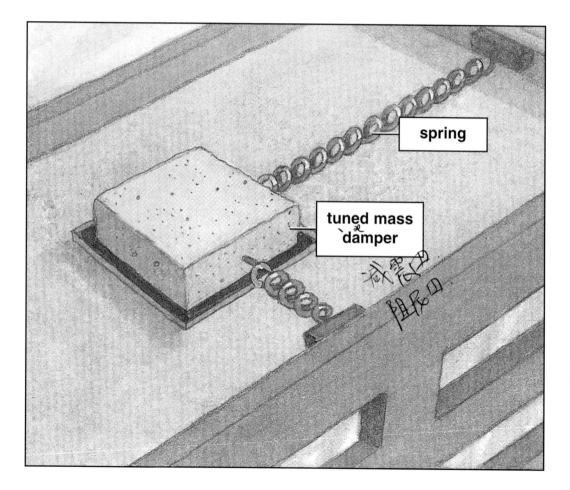

spring

tuned mass damper

My, How You've Grown!

The world's first skyscraper, the Home Insurance Building, was only ten storeys high. Built more than 100 years ago in Chicago, U.S.A., it was the first multi-storey building constructed with a steel framework. Since then, many skyscrapers built in a similar way have become world famous for their heights.

In the next few years, the record for the tallest office building in the world will be challenged by a new office tower in Asia. With its scheduled completion in 2001, the Universal Financial Centre in Shanghai, China, will be 2.1 metres taller than the Petronas Towers in Malaysia. Plans are being made to build an even taller tower in Seoul, Korea.

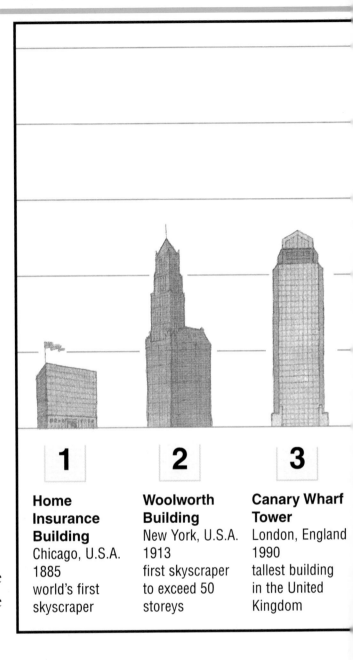

1

Home Insurance Building
Chicago, U.S.A.
1885
world's first skyscraper

2

Woolworth Building
New York, U.S.A.
1913
first skyscraper to exceed 50 storeys

3

Canary Wharf Tower
London, England
1990
tallest building in the United Kingdom

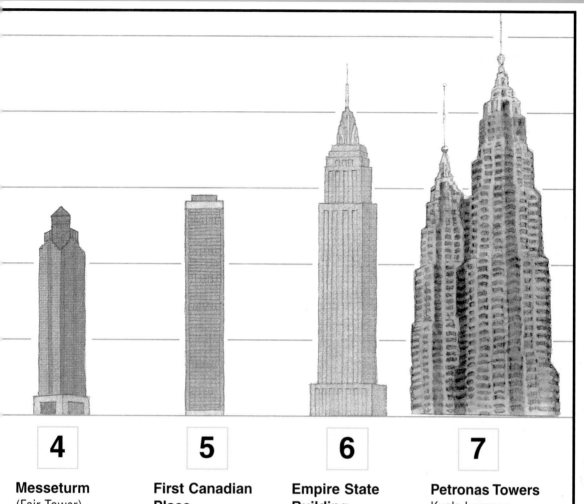

4

Messeturm
(Fair Tower)
Frankfurt, Germany
1990
tallest building in
Europe

5

**First Canadian
Place**
Toronto, Canada
1975
built at a rate of three
storeys a week

6

**Empire State
Building**
New York, U.S.A.
1931
first skyscraper to
exceed 100 storeys

7

Petronas Towers
Kuala Lumpur,
Malaysia
1996
tallest office building
in the world

AFTER YOU READ

Compare graphics and text

How did the graphics help you understand the
information better?

High Flyers:

Making Paper Airplanes

Written by Bob Bonnet and Dan Keen
Illustrated by Kim LaFave

READING TIP

Follow instructions

Authors give directions by using action words that tell you exactly what to do. As you read, look for the action word in each step.

When you make a paper airplane, the goal is a plane that will stay in the air a long time before gravity pulls it down. Does wing shape make a difference? What about the material used to make the plane?

Make three paper airplanes using the same design. Instructions for a popular design are given on the following pages, or you can use a design of your own. Make one plane using regular paper, one out of aluminum foil, and one out of wax paper. Which plane stays in the air the longest?

Experiment with different airplane designs using the three different types of material. A design that works best for the aluminum plane might not work well for the plane made out of wax paper.

LEARNING GOALS

You will

- find out how to make a paper airplane
- learn how authors make instructions easy to follow

Do the planes fly better when there is a wind? Should you launch the planes into the wind, or with the wind behind you? Do you get better flights if you just toss the planes easily, or if you throw them harder, trying to make them go farther?

Paper Airplane Design

You will need:

- a sheet of writing paper
- a piece of wax paper
- a piece of aluminum foil

1. Fold a sheet of writing paper in half lengthwise and crease it.

2. Open up and flatten the sheet.

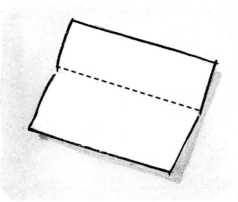

3. At one end, fold both corners down, lining edges up with the centre crease.

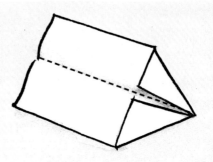

4. Fold each corner edge down again, against the centre fold, and crease well. Fold in the sharp point, for safety.

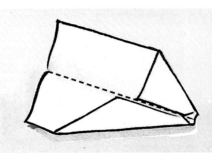

5. Turn the paper over.

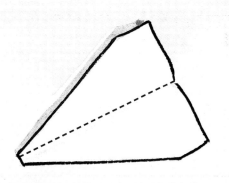

6. Fold the two outer edges back into the creased centre line.

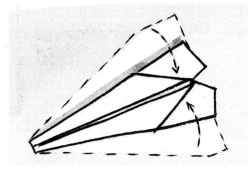

7. Fold the plane together and crease all folds well.

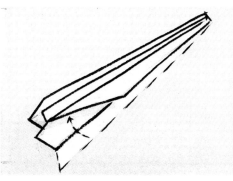

8. Bend the wings out into position and test fly your plane.

AFTER YOU READ

Make a list

Make a list of the action words that helped you follow the instructions. How else did the author make the instructions easy to follow?

Building an Igloo

Written and photographed by Ulli Steltzer

READING TIP

Read pictures

A photo essay gives information through pictures.
Look carefully at the pictures as you read the text.
They will help you to understand what you read.

Winter in the Northern Arctic is long and cold—so long that by September the ocean starts to freeze over, and so cold that the ice soon forms a cover two metres deep. No wonder, then, that any moisture in the air freezes right away. On cloudy days it may come down as snow; on clear days the air is full of tiny, silvery ice crystals. A new layer of white covers land and sea every day, packing down hard in some places and settling loosely in others.

LEARNING GOALS

You will

- find out how an igloo is made
- use pictures to get information

Trees have never grown in this part of the world. For centuries the people of the Arctic, the Inuit, built their houses of snow. They called them igloo in some regions, though others used different words, such as "igluviak". Snow was everywhere, and the only tool needed was a knife of bone, antler, or walrus tusk.

Depending on the size of the family, its igloo was big or small. Even giant igloos were built as places to dance to the sound of drums. Both light and heat were provided by a stone lamp (called a *kuliq*) burning seal fat and using the cotton-like seeds of a small plant for a wick. Of course, each igloo needed a chimney where hot air could escape, or the whole top would begin to melt.

When many people lived in an igloo, they sometimes damaged its walls. Rather than continually patching their igloo, the family would build a new one. Often an igloo was abandoned because the family moved to better hunting grounds, leaving their old house to melt away in the summer sun.

Tookillkee Kiguktak lives in Griese Fiord, the most northern settlement in Canada, on Ellesmere Island. He does not live in an igloo; like all the Inuit of today he lives in a house. But when Tookillkee was a little child he lived in an igloo, and when he was a boy he learned how to build one. Ever since, when he goes hunting far away for a musk ox or a polar bear, he builds an igloo for shelter.

A hunter never goes alone on a long trip. Tookillkee likes to take along Jopee, one of his four sons, and of course Jopee—like his father—long ago learned how to build an igloo.

It takes several hours of hard work to build a good igloo. The most important thing is to find the right kind of snow. Not too soft, not too hard.

Tookillkee starts walking over the land. Only when the surface remains unbroken under his feet does he stop. With his carpenter saw, he checks the depth and quality of the snow. On a rocky slope, like the site shown here, he has to be especially careful to find a large enough area of good snow. Once he has found it, he steps to one side of the good snow and paces off a circle. This is where he will build his igloo.

Tookillkee outlines the blocks in the snow before he cuts them. Then, with the blade of the saw, he lifts up each one. It can weigh from eight to twelve kilograms depending on size.

He lines up the blocks alongside the growing trench from which they were cut.

When he has cut all the blocks, it is time to start building the igloo.

He cuts diagonally into the blocks to start a spiral.

Jopee helps with the carrying. Before bringing a fresh block, he waits until his father has set the last one in position.

After setting each block, Tookillkee trims and cleans its surface with a long knife.

The final blocks that round off the top need skillful shaping and fitting.

Tookillkee reaches up and places the last block, the keystone of the igloo. He is locked in.

With his knife he cuts a low doorway and crawls out.

After Tookillkee and Jopee fill in the cracks with soft snow, Tookillkee builds a chimney.

Tookillkee decides to build a porch. It will keep the cold draft from coming inside and will give him storage space, especially for food, boots, and bulky clothing. He cuts more snow blocks. After attaching the first two rows to both sides of the igloo's entrance, he rounds off the top on the gentle slope of a spiral. No chimney is needed for the porch, and the cracks are filled in quickly.

The igloo is ready.

It is evening. Father and son settle down inside. They look out on the frozen ocean. Tomorrow will be a day of hunting.

AFTER YOU READ

Compare pictures and text

How did the pictures help you understand the text?

Kids Talk About Building

Written by Norma Kennedy

READING TIP

Think about what you already know

Writers explain how to make something by using order words like "next," "then," "first," and "last." As you read, note the steps in building these different structures.

If you have ever made a paper airplane, followed a recipe, stitched a puppet, made a fort, or used building blocks, you have created something—you have put things together to make something else.

Builders make things by doing things in a certain order. Maybe you tried a few different ways to build what you made before you got it just right.

Here are some children who have made things and want to tell about them!

Joshua talks about building a house of cards.

The first time I tried to build a house with cards, I tried to make a square. When I got about four cards together, they all fell down.

So I tried leaning them together so they made triangles. That worked better.

LEARNING GOALS

You will

- find out how different structures are made
- learn how using order words helps you follow the steps

Shaina talks about building a camera and tripod.

I started with boxes of different sizes and shapes, and some tubes and cups and things like that. Some of the shapes made me think of a camera, so I thought I'd build a camera of the future.

First, I taped two of the same kind of boxes together. The top one has the viewfinder. Then I used different-sized cardboard tubes to make the lens.

Next, I attached the long lens to the camera part. I cut a hole in the back and fit the tubes in, but it was too heavy in the front. So I built a base for it to stand on. I wanted to build a tripod, but I couldn't get three legs to hold together right so I just used two.

Last, I used shoe boxes for the base because they were the sturdiest. The base had to be sturdy so the camera could stand by itself and so that I could move it.

Now look at the camera and say, "Pizza!"

Kyle talks about building with blocks.

To make this building, here's what I did:
First, I made a solid base of square blue blocks.

Next, I put the long red rectangles on top of the blue ones on both sides of the base. Then I put a bridge across the space in the middle and arches at either end.

I used some of the cylinders to build up higher, then put rectangle blocks across them. I discovered that I could put two triangles together to make a rectangle, so I had more flat shapes to build on.

Then I used other cylinders to build up even higher.

Last, I balanced two short blocks across the cylinders. The last one was the hardest to put on.

Caroline talks about building a rocket out of straws and connectors.

This is how I made the rocket:

1. First, I made a square out of eight straws, two straws on each side.
2. Then, I made seven more squares just like it—all the same size.
3. I built the top part onto one square. First I used one straw on each corner but it looked too squished. So I used two straws at each corner and joined them in the middle. That made it higher and pointier. Now the top is sort of like a cone.
4. I joined one square to another with eight more straws.
5. I joined all eight squares together the same way. I had to put the rocket on its side when it got too high for me to reach.

106

6. Then I stood the rocket up so the cone was at the top. But it was too wiggly and I was afraid it would collapse.
7. So I put straws in a "†" across the inside of four of the sections. They brace the sides to hold them apart.

Now it's ready for blast off!

Jonathon talks about building a submarine.

I started putting Lego™ pieces together to make the bottom of my submarine. Then I had to fix it because it was tipping side-to-side all the time. I made it flatter by overlapping the pieces more so they wouldn't tip.

When I was building the sides, I left space in the middle so the captain could walk from one end of the submarine to the other without going outside.

After I'd made the main part of the submarine, I put an escape pod on at the back. Then I put skis on the bottom so it could go up on the beach sometimes. And there's a diver cage, too.

AFTER YOU READ

Write a paragraph

Write what you have learned about building with shapes.

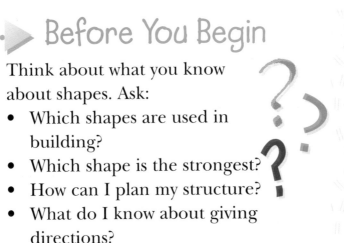

UNIT 2 WRAP-UP

Engineer It!

In this unit, you read about shapes and how shapes are used in building things. Now you'll use what you've learned about shapes to build the tallest cardboard structure you can. Then you will show your classmates how to build a structure just like yours.

⟩ Before You Begin

Think about what you know about shapes. Ask:

- Which shapes are used in building?
- Which shape is the strongest?
- How can I plan my structure?
- What do I know about giving directions?
- Who will be the audience for my presentation?
- How will I remember my presentation?

What Supplies Will I Need?

- tape
- scissors
- cardboard rectangles (e.g., sports cards, flash cards)

Here is Michael's plan for his structure.

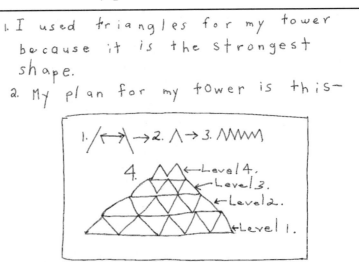

1. I used triangles for my tower because it is the strongest shape.
2. My plan for my tower is this—

1. /↔\ → 2. ∧ → 3. ⋀⋀⋀⋀⋀
4. ⋀⋀⋀ ←Level 4.
←Level 3.
←Level 2.
←Level 1.

Make Your Structure

1 **Construct it.**

- As you make your paper structure, stop and make notes after each step.
- Draw diagrams to help you remember each step.

2 **Test it.**

- Build your structure one more time, following the steps you have written.
- Revise and change any notes or diagrams.

3 **Write the first draft of your presentation.**

- Review your notes.
- Write out the steps, starting with the first thing you did.

To help you remember what you want to say, list your steps on note cards.

Here are some of Michael's steps.

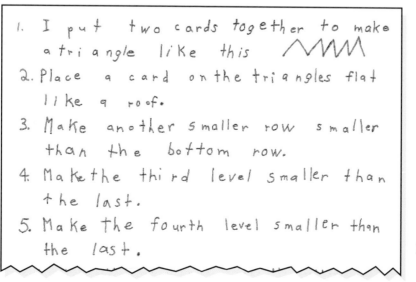

1. I put two cards together to make a triangle like this ∧∧∧∧
2. Place a card on the triangles flat like a roof.
3. Make another smaller row smaller than the bottom row.
4. Make the third level smaller than the last.
5. Make the fourth level smaller than the last.

109

Practise Your Presentation

When you tell others how to do something, you have to:

1. Learn the directions. Read them over a few times.
2. Practise saying the directions out loud without looking at your notes.
3. Practise the presentation, having a classmate build the structure while you give the directions.
4. Finish the presentation by sharing what you learned about shapes and building things.

Think About Your Audience

- Use posters or pictures.
- Use action words.
- Pick a volunteer to help you.
- Don't speak too fast.
- Look at your classmates.

Here is one stage of Michael's structure.

Revise and Edit

Before you make your presentation, ask yourself:
- Did I read through my directions?
- Did I practise by reading my directions to someone else?
- Do my directions make sense?

Revise and edit anything you want to change and then practise making your presentation again.

...▶ Present It

There are different ways to make your presentation.

- Videotape a helper building the structure and talk about what is on the tape.
- Use a poster that shows the steps to follow.
- Have more than one classmate try to build the structure following your directions.

...▶ Think About Your Learning

- Did you make the presentation interesting?
- Did you use order words?
- Did you give enough time for the builder to complete each step?
- Did you let them ask questions?
- Did you learn new things about shapes?

Unit 3: *Good Books, Good Times!*

Poems! Stories! Folktales! Although stories and poems are all quite different, you will see how they often have similar features. You will look for settings, problems and solutions, and clues about characters. You will learn how folktales often contain a message or lesson for the reader. You will

- compare features of poems and stories
- look for words that describe setting
- use clues to figure out new words
- make a chart to show a story's problem and the character's solution
- write your own story

Good Books, Good Times!

Written by Lee Bennett Hopkins
Illustrated by Scot Ritchie

READING TIP

Think about what you already know

Make a list of what you know about poems. As you read, look for these features as well as other features that these poets use.

Good books.
Good times.
Good stories.
Good rhymes.
Good beginnings.
Good ends.
Good people.
Good friends.

Good fiction.
Good facts.
Good adventures.
Good acts.
Good stories.
Good rhymes.
Good books.
Good times.

The Reason I Like Chocolate

Written by Nikki Giovanni
Illustrated by Norman Eyolfson

The reason I like chocolate
is I can lick my fingers
and nobody tells me I'm not polite

I especially like scary movies
'cause I can snuggle with Mommy
or my big sister and they don't laugh

I like to cry sometimes 'cause
everybody says 'what's the matter
don't cry'

and I like books for all those reasons
but mostly 'cause they just make me
happy

and I really like
to be happy

AFTER YOU READ

Make a chart

Make a chart comparing the two poems and what
special features the poets used.

Special Feature	Good Books, Good Times!	The Reason I Like Chocolate
rhyme		

Hold On, McGinty!

Written by Nancy Hartry
Illustrated by Don Kilby

READING TIP

Think about the setting

Where this story takes place is an important part of the story. As you read, think about the words the author uses to help you experience the setting.

Every morning, Old McGinty woke up before it was light and picked his way down the stony trail from his house to the sea.

Every morning, he greeted his fishing dory, the *Heart's Content*. "Good morning, my girl," and he shoved the yellowed stern out into the salty spray.

And every day for over sixty years, the old boat and the old man caught fathoms of fish.

Until one morning, there was hardly a nibble.

"Where are the fish?" McGinty asked the *Heart's Content.*

He rowed way, way out into the bay. He heaved the sodden net overboard and then stood at the prow of his boat. For luck, he belted out two songs: *"Oh Can-a-da,"* and then his very own, very proud version *"Oh New-found-land."*

When the sun was low in the sky, he pulled in the gill net, hand over hand over hand. Only a few slippery fish sluiced into the bottom of the boat.

McGinty rowed back and beached the *Heart's Content*. He collected some driftwood, built a fire, and boiled a codfish for breakfast. The blackened teapot burbled on the coals.

"Ahh...," he sighed, and he said thanks to Canada and to Newfoundland.

But the next day, when McGinty rowed out, he caught no fish at all. And he had no real breakfast.

The next day he rowed farther.

No fish. No breakfast!

"My stomach is growling," McGinty said to the *Heart's Content.*

"How are you feeling, m'dear?"

The boat pressed on.

Day after day. Week after week. He rowed farther and still no fish. Just one tiny flounder that he threw back into the sea.

McGinty pulled the *Heart's Content* out of the water, left her resting on the rocks. Turtled.

Now, every other night, McGinty's telephone rang at precisely nine o'clock.

"That'll be the granddaughter.... Luv'ly to hear from you, Molly!" He closed his eyes and waited for the dreaded question.

"Move to Vancouver Island?" he asked. "Ridiculous! Molly ... Molly ... I don't care if they are catching fish as big as cows in Cowichan Bay. My home is here. You're not to worry. I have *so* been catching fish. I miss you too, my love."

McGinty could not sleep. He put on his red corduroy slippers and his plaid wool robe and scuffled down the stony trail to talk to the *Heart's Content.*

McGinty paced up and down. "I am hungry," he said. "And look at you, my girl—you're peeling and drying out."

He sat on a rock. "You are old and I am old. We have been together a long time. What shall we do?"

"I did have one little idea I've been keeping from you." McGinty pulled out the globe hidden under his bathrobe. "I want to discuss it." He spun the world around and measured the distance from St. John's, Newfoundland, to Victoria, British Columbia, with the span of his great hand.

"It's not so far, twenty-five centimetres is all. We can do it. We must do it. We need to fish!"

McGinty sent a telegram to his granddaughter:

GOING ON A LONG LONG VOYAGE STOP
WILL CALL WHEN I DOCK STOP

Then McGinty telephoned the train station on the mainland.

He boarded up the house. He scraped the traces of barnacles off the *Heart's Content*. He rubbed her and painted her until she gleamed. He mounted a compass in the bow. "You're going on a long and tremendous voyage," said McGinty. "We must make you sound."

McGinty walked away, and then turned back. "I know this is the first time you and I have been apart, but I cannot go with you. You are freight and I'm a passenger. You'll be fine on that train. Don't be afraid."

He knelt down, filled the old teapot to the brim with Atlantic seawater, and set it gently in the bottom of the *Heart's Content*.

McGinty blew his nose on his white handkerchief and cleared his throat. "I will wait for you half way, m'dear—if that would be quite all right with you."

He patted the *Heart's Content* and wished her good day and good luck.

One last time, McGinty picked his way along the stony trail from his house to the sea. As the sun was setting over the bay at Come-by-Chance, McGinty sang only one song: *"Ode to Newfoundland."*

McGinty flew directly to Toronto and stayed in the only hotel he knew. He looked out the window with his spyglass, waiting for the *Heart's Content*.

Every evening, he telephoned the train station.

"Is she here yet?" he asked the stationmaster. "What's her position, laddie?" He charted her course on the map he'd tacked to the hotel room wall.

By the fifth day, McGinty was in great distress. "Is she lost? At sea? We've never been apart—I must set eyes on her!"

"It's against the rules," growled the stationmaster. Then he whispered, "She departs Toronto tonight."

Old McGinty checked out of the hotel. He bought a sleeping bag, some warm woollen socks, red flannel underwear, fresh water, and a case of canned mackerel.

He hurried to the rail terminal. He limped along the gravel of Track Number Three as fast as his land legs would take him. Past rail cars of coal and plywood. Coils of steel. Giant rolls of newsprint.

He crossed to Track Two and searched from caboose to engine. No boat.

"Where are you, girl?" Then he spied her, sidelined all alone.

McGinty removed his cap and bowed low from the waist. "Good evening, m'dear," he said to the *Heart's Content.* "My, my—you're drier than a salt cod." He sprinkled some water from the old teapot onto her hull, and rubbed it in.

Then, McGinty quietly, stealthily, stowed away his gear—and himself!

He braced his feet on the port gunwale and rested his head on a lifebuoy at starboard. He battened down the tarpaulin.

"Snug as a bug in a rug!" said McGinty.

Stowaway McGinty turned night into day.

He straddled the prow of his ship and navigated by the stars. He watched the endless shadows of forest roll past.

The moon was low in the sky, shining across the islands of Lake Superior. The Northern Lights shivered in the sky and on the water.

Across the Prairies, he poked up his head like a gopher, and rowed the waves of golden grain.

Up and over, up and over the ripples of the Alberta foothills.

"Brace y'self, missy," warned Captain McGinty. "There's heavy weather ahead."

And sure enough, the *Heart's Content* bobbed and bounced through the heave and ho of the Rocky Mountains ...

... over the Fraser Canyon ...

... and came to rest, shunted at the Strait of Georgia.

"Almost there, m'girl," whispered Captain McGinty. "Can you taste the salt of the Pacific Ocean?"

The *Heart's Content* rolled onto a ferry bound for Vancouver Island.

On this last leg of the voyage, Captain McGinty threw back the tarpaulin. "Whales to the portside!" he called happily. "Sea otters and seals north by northwest. Land Ho-*oh*!"

Captain McGinty watched eagerly as the *Heart's Content* was lowered into the water. He took an oar and splashed her until she was slippery and shining.

He pulled on his sou'wester and his big rubber boots and out from his pockets came maps and charts.

"It's not by chance that I come by Cowichan!" McGinty shouted at the stars.

He baited his hooks with canned mackerel from the Grand Banks, and trolled as the sun came up. He hauled a Spring salmon into his little dory.

"This one's for my darlin' Molly. It's as big and shiny as a codfish!" he cried. He hauled in another and another. "Hold on there, McGinty!"

Captain McGinty rowed back to shore. He gathered driftwood, built a fire, and fried a salmon for breakfast.

"Canada is a great and glorious land," he sighed, "and ten provinces is more than twenty-five centimetres!" Then he sang a new song: *"Oh, Bri-tish Co-lum-bia!"*

The song sounded out of tune.

Captain McGinty knelt down at the water's edge and emptied the water of the Atlantic Ocean into the water of the Pacific Ocean. Then he belted out a prayer of hope for the fish of Newfoundland.

That prayer blew with the westerly winds across the Strait of Georgia, over the Fraser Canyon, bobbed and bounced through the Rocky Mountains, up and over the ripples of the Alberta foothills, across the Prairies to Toronto, where it was blown off course to Ottawa, then, shooting down the roiling rivers of Quebec, sailed straight on, jiggity jig, all the way to Newfoundland.

"Hold on!" whispered McGinty.

AFTER YOU READ

Make a list of describing words

Look back at the story. What words does the author use to make you experience the places McGinty visited on his trip to the West?

Sam and the Lucky Money

Written by Karen Chinn
Illustrated by Cornelius Van Wright and Ying-Hwa Hu

READING TIP

Think about the problem

Stories often begin with a character who has a problem. The story gets more and more interesting as the character tries different ways to solve the problem. As you read this story, think about Sam's problem, and see if you can predict how he will solve it.

Sam could hardly wait to get going. He zipped up his jacket and patted his pockets. It was time to go to Chinatown for New Year's Day!

Sam thought about sweet oranges and "lucky money": Crisp dollar bills tucked in small red envelopes called *leisees*.

Sam's grandparents gave him leisees every New Year. Each envelope was decorated with a symbol of luck: Two golden mandarins. A Chinese junk. A slithering dragon. A giant peach. Sam's leisees were embossed in gold.

Sam counted out four dollars. Boy, did he feel rich! His parents said he didn't have to buy a notebook or socks as usual. This year he could spend his lucky money *his* way.

"Sam!" his mother called. "It's time to go shopping. Hurry, so we don't miss the lion!"

"Coming!" said Sam.

The streets hummed with the thump of drums and the clang of cymbals. Everywhere dusty red smoke hung in the air left by exploding firecrackers.

"Give me your hand," said his mother. "I don't want you to get lost." Sam took her hand reluctantly. It seemed like everyone was shopping for the New Year's meals. There were so many people crowded around the overflowing vegetable bins that Sam had to look out for elbows and shopping bags.

Right next to the vegetable stand were two huge red-paper mounds. Sam kicked the piles with his right foot, and then with his left foot, until he created a small blizzard. On his third kick he felt his foot land on something strange.

"Aiya!" someone cried out in pain.

Startled, he looked up to find an old man sitting against the wall. The stranger was rubbing his foot. *Bare feet in winter!* Sam thought. *Where are his shoes?*

Sam stared at the man's dirty clothes as he backed away. He found his mother picking out oranges and he tugged on her sleeve, pulling harder than he meant to.

"Hey, I need this arm," she said. "Where have you been? It's time to go."

For once, Sam was glad to follow his mother.

In the bakery window, Sam eyed a gleaming row of fresh *char siu bao,* his favourite honey-topped buns. When they opened the door, the smell of sweet egg tarts and coconut pastries erased any thought of the stranger. Sam wondered how many sweets he could buy with four dollars.

"Nay yu mat yeh ah?" said a young woman from behind the counter. When Sam gave her a puzzled look, she repeated the question in English. "What do you want?"

Sam was about to ask for buns when he noticed a tray full of New Year's cookies. They were shaped like fish, with fat, pleated tails that looked like little toes. He couldn't help but think about the old man again. Sam decided he wasn't hungry after all.

Suddenly, he heard a noise from outside that sounded like a thousand leaves rustling. He ran to the window to see what was happening.

"Look!" he yelled. Bundles of firecrackers were exploding in the street. Rounding the corner was the festival lion, followed by a band of cymbals and drums. Sam pulled his mother outside.

The colourful lion wove down the street like a giant centipede. Teased by a clown wearing a round mask, it tossed its head up and down.

It came to a halt in front of a meat market, and sniffed a giant leisee that hung in the doorway, along with a bouquet of lettuce leaves. With loud fanfare, the band urged the lion toward its prize.

"Take the food! Take the money! Bring us good luck for the New Year!" Sam shouted along with the others. His heart pounded in time with the drum's beat. With a sudden lunge, the lion devoured the leisee all in an eye-blink and continued down the street. The crowd clapped and then quickly dispersed.

"That was a hungry lion," Sam's mother joked. Now he felt hungry too, and wanted to go back to the bakery.

But just then, a large "Grand Opening" sign caught Sam's eye. In the window were cars, planes, robots, and stuffed animals. A new toy store! Just the place to spend his lucky money!

Sam ran down one aisle, then another. He examined a police car with a wailing siren and flashing lights. He squeezed a talking pig and laughed at its loud "Oink, oink!" Then, he spotted the basketballs.

A new basketball was the perfect way to spend his lucky money. But when he saw the price tag, he got angry.

"I only have four dollars," he shouted. "I can't buy this." In fact, everything he touched cost more than that.

"What is four dollars good for?" he complained, stamping his feet. His mother scrunched up her eyes, the way she always did when she scolded him, and guided him out the door.

Sam couldn't help it. Even with all the shiny gold on them, the leisees seemed worthless.

"Sam, when someone gives you something, you should appreciate it," his mother said as she marched him along. Sam stuffed his leisees back in his pockets. The sun had disappeared behind some clouds, and he was starting to feel the chill. He dragged his feet along the sidewalk.

Suddenly, Sam saw a pair of bare feet, and instantly recognized them. They belonged to the old man he had seen earlier. The man also remembered him, and smiled. Sam froze in his steps, staring at the man's feet.

His mother kept walking. When she turned back to check on Sam, she noticed the old man. "Oh," she said, shifting her shopping bags so she could dig in her purse for some coins. "Sorry—I only have a quarter." The man bowed his head several times in thanks.

He acts like it's a million bucks, Sam thought, shaking his head. As they started to walk away, Sam looked down at his own feet, warm and dry in his boots. Suddenly he stopped.

"Can I really do anything I want with my lucky money?" he asked.

"Yes, of course," his mother answered.

Sam pulled his leisees from his pockets. The golden dragon looked shinier than ever. He ran back and thrust his lucky money into the surprised man's hands.

"You can't buy shoes with this," he told the man, "but I know you can buy some socks." The stranger laughed, and so did Sam's mother.

Sam walked back to his mother and took her warm hand. She smiled and gave a gentle squeeze. And as they headed home for more New Year's celebration, Sam knew he was the lucky one.

AFTER YOU READ

Solve the problem

What was Sam's problem? Use a chart like the one below to show some of the solutions Sam thought of and how he finally solved his problem.

Sam's Problem	Sam Tried	What Happened

A Lion in the Meadow

Written by Margaret Mahy
Illustrated by Blanche Sims

READING TIP

Think about stories you know

Authors write stories about things that could really happen and stories that are imaginary or fantasy. As you read, what clues does the author give to tell you what kind of story this is?

The little boy said, "Mother, there is a lion in the meadow."

The mother said, "Nonsense, little boy."

The little boy said, "Mother, there is a big yellow lion in the meadow."

The mother said, "Nonsense, little boy."

The little boy said, "Mother, there is a big, roaring, yellow, whiskery lion in the meadow!"

The mother said, "Little boy, you are making up stories again. There is nothing in the meadow but grass and trees. Go into the meadow and see for yourself."

The little boy said, "Mother, I'm scared to go into the meadow, because of the lion which is there."

The mother said, "Little boy, you are making up stories—so I will make up a story, too.... Do you see this matchbox? Take it out into the meadow and open it. In it will be a tiny dragon. The tiny dragon will grow into a big dragon. It will chase the lion away."

The little boy took the matchbox and went away. The mother went on peeling the potatoes.

Suddenly the door opened.

In rushed a big, roaring, yellow, whiskery lion.

"Hide me!" it said. "A dragon is after me!"

The lion hid in the broom cupboard.

Then the little boy came running in.

"Mother," he said. "That dragon grew too big. There is no lion in the meadow now. There is a DRAGON in the meadow."

The little boy hid in the broom cupboard too.

"You should have left me alone," said the lion. "I eat only apples."

"But there wasn't a real dragon," said the mother. "It was just a story I made up."

"It turned out to be true after all," said the little boy. "You should have looked in the matchbox first."

"That is how it is," said the lion. "Some stories are true, and some aren't.... But I have an idea. We will go and play in the meadow on the other side of the house. There is no dragon there."

"I am glad we are friends now," said the little boy.

The little boy and the big roaring yellow whiskery lion went to play in the other meadow. The dragon stayed where he was, and nobody minded.

The mother never ever made up a story again.

AFTER YOU READ

Make a Chart

Make a chart that describes the parts of the story that could be real, and the parts that were fantasy.

Could really happen	Fantasy

Two Pairs of Shoes

Written by Esther Sanderson
Illustrated by David Beyer

READING TIP

Think about your experiences

Have you ever received something from a special person that has special meaning for you? Read to find out about the special gifts the girl in this story receives.

"Look what I bought, *nitanis*," Maggie's mother said, holding out a box, for it was Maggie's eighth birthday.

"What is it?" asked Maggie.

"Look in and find out," said her mother.

Maggie's heart was pounding as she took the box into her hands. She hoped, but didn't dare believe, that in the box would be the thing she had been waiting for.

LEARNING GOALS

You will

- read about a girl who receives a special gift from her grandmother

- find out how thinking about your own life can help you understand story characters

She looked in the box and inside were the most beautiful shoes she'd ever seen—black, patent leather shoes! They were the ones she had seen at Fowler's Store. She had been dreaming of these shoes ever since she saw them in the store that spring. Maggie quickly tore off her moccasins and slid her feet into the black leather shoes. They fit perfectly!

Down the road she ran to show off her beautiful new shoes to her *Kokom*. She hardly even felt the ground beneath her as she floated down the gravel road.

When she arrived at her *Kokom*'s house, she was sitting in her favourite chair in the corner of her kitchen.

"Look *Kokom*, I have new shoes," said Maggie, her little face beaming.

"Come *nosisim*, and let me feel them," said her *Kokom*, for Maggie's *Kokom* was blind and could only see by touching.

Kokom felt the shoes all over, while Maggie stood silently watching her.

"They're very nice, *nosisim*," said *Kokom* handing Maggie back her new shoes.

"Now go to the box that I keep under my

bed and bring out the bag that's in there." The box that *Kokom* kept under her bed was opened only on special occasions. It was known to Maggie, her sisters, and her brothers as the "special box." As Maggie looked under the bed she wondered what would be in the special box for her today. She brought the paper bag to her *Kokom*.

"Open it, *nosisim*," said *Kokom.* Maggie opened up the bag and inside was a pair of moccasins. They were beaded in the most beautiful flower designs that Maggie had ever seen. Tears came to her eyes as she suddenly remembered her *Kokom* couldn't see. How could she have made such a beautiful pair of moccasins?

"Well *nosisim*," said *Kokom,* "today is a special day for you, for you have been given two pairs of shoes. From now on you must remember when and how to wear each pair."

AFTER YOU READ

Write about your own life

Think about a special gift you have received from someone. Write a paragraph telling what the gift meant to you.

Anansi and Turtle
An Ashanti Tale

Retold by Rita Cox
Illustrated by Joe Weissmann

READING TIP

Find out about folktales

A folktale is a story that has been told over and over for many years. What do you already know about folktales? What messages do they have? As you read, find out the message of this folktale.

Anansi the Spider was a greedy fellow. Everybody in the village knew about his great appetite.

One day, Anansi cooked a fine meal of fish and yams for his dinner. Oh! It smelled so delicious! It made Anansi's mouth water. He could not wait to enjoy his tasty meal.

Just as Anansi was getting ready to eat, there was a knock on his door. A stranger was standing there. His name was Turtle. The appetizing aroma had drawn him to Anansi's house.

"I come from far away. I have been travelling all day in the heat and the dust, and am tired and hungry. Would you share your meal with me?"

Greedy Anansi wanted to eat his food all by himself, but in his country, there was a rule that strangers must be treated with kindness, and shown hospitality. He had to invite Turtle into his house and share his meal with him.

Even though he didn't want to, Anansi smiled and said, "Come in, Turtle. I would be happy to share my dinner with you."

But Anansi had a plan.

Turtle went up to the table. As he reached hungrily to help himself from the dishes, Anansi said to him, "Your hands are awfully dirty. It is not good manners to come to the table without first washing your hands. Please go to the stream at the bottom of the hill and wash yourself."

Turtle went to the stream, washed his hands and feet, and climbed back up the hill to Anansi's house. He was hungrier than ever.

Anansi had already eaten half of the meal, when Turtle went up to the table again and reached for the food once more. But his hands and feet were covered with dirt from the walk up the hill.

"Turtle," said Anansi angrily, "your hands are still dirty. Please respect my table, and go and wash them again."

Turtle was ashamed. "Oh," he replied. "It is the dust from my journey up the hill."

Disappointed and weak with hunger, Turtle returned to the stream, washed his hands and feet again, and returned to the house. This time he was careful to walk on the grass at the side of the hill.

Turtle hurried to the table, only to find that the dishes were empty. Anansi had eaten up all the food.

"What a tasty meal that was!" said Anansi, licking his lips. "Wasn't it, Turtle?"

Sad as he was, Turtle smiled. "Yes, Anansi. Thank you for your kindness. If you ever come to my village, be sure to visit me and share a meal with me." Turtle said goodbye and went on his way.

Many months later, Anansi travelled to Turtle's village. After awhile, he found Turtle resting on the riverbank, soaking up the sun.

Seeing Anansi, Turtle greeted him cheerfully. "Ah, Anansi! Welcome to my village. You have come a long way. I am sure that you are tired and hungry. Would you like to join me for dinner?"

"Oh yes, I would," replied Anansi eagerly. "I have been looking forward to your hospitality."

"Good," said Turtle. "I'll go and prepare our meal."

Turtle slipped into the water, and dived to his home at the bottom of the river. He set out the food. It looked and smelled delicious.

Anansi was growing hungrier and hungrier, and was pleased when Turtle reappeared and announced, "Dinner is ready. Please join me, Anansi."

Anansi followed Turtle into the water, but because his body was so light, he floated to the top again and again. He dived, he splashed, he kicked, he jumped. Try as he would, he could not reach the bottom of the river where Turtle was, sitting at his table enjoying his dinner.

Anansi's stomach hurt. He must have some of Turtle's delicious food. He thought and thought. Then he had an idea. From the riverbank he gathered pebbles. He filled the pockets of his jacket with them.

Then he dived into the river. Success! The pebbles made him heavy enough to sink to the bottom.

There was Turtle enjoying the delicious spread that he had prepared. He had already eaten half of it.

The sight and smell of the food made Anansi lick his lips. He sat at Turtle's table and reached for the delicious food.

Just as Anansi was about to eat, Turtle said to him, "I must tell you, my friend, that in my country it is not polite to wear our jackets to the table. Please remove yours."

Turtle took another mouthful while Anansi removed his jacket and reached for the food once more. But, without the weight of the pebbles, Anansi could not stay on the river bottom, and floated up to the top of the water.

Meanwhile, Turtle finished eating all the food, then paddled up to the riverbank where a hungry Anansi sat, looking very sad.

"Anansi, my friend," said Turtle. "Wasn't that a wonderful dinner? It was a pleasure to have you as my guest. Please come again soon."

AFTER YOU READ

Write the message of the story

In your own words, write the message of this folktale.

Author Talk

Written by Trudee Romanek

What makes a story a good story? What makes it a story you want to read again and again?

One way to find out is to ask the people who write them. I talked to three Canadian authors to find out how they write children's stories. Here's what they said.

Jan Bourdeau Waboose

Trudee: What kind of stories do you write?
Jan: My stories are about Native culture and traditions.

Trudee: How do you begin writing your stories?
Jan: I'll think about an adventure I had as a child. That adventure will be the starting point for my story.

Trudee: Do you write the whole story at once?

Jan: Yes. I write until the character's story is told. Then, I type it into my computer and put it away for a few days. When I have gathered some new ideas, I take it out and add those.

Trudee: What makes a good story?

Jan: A good story is one that describes what the character sees, smells, hears, feels, even tastes. If a writer uses all five senses, it draws readers in, right from the very first page.

Trudee: What tips would you give to young writers?

Jan: Write about your own thoughts and feelings, about things you do or dream of doing. Pay attention to everything around you. Even a dragonfly buzzing overhead has a story to tell.

Tololwa M. Mollel

Trudee: What kind of stories do you write?

Tololwa: Most people call what I write folktales. I take a story that I have heard and I tell it in my own way, with my own words. Sometimes I add things, sometimes I leave out things.

Trudee: How do you begin writing your stories?

Tololwa: I get an idea, something that excites me. It could be a character's name, an image, an event, something like that. I let it knock around in my head for awhile. Since the story is one I have heard, the *plot*, or what happens next, is already there. I have to decide what I will change to make it a story that I think is good.

Trudee: Do you write the whole story at once?

Tololwa: No, I work on one section at a time. To me, the beginning of a story is the hardest part. I write the beginning many different ways. I try again and again until I am happy with it. Only then do I begin to write the next part of the story. When I have written the whole story on paper, I go back and type it all. I often make some changes while I am typing too.

Trudee: What makes a good story?
Tololwa: Most stories are about people who aren't real. A good story can make its characters seem real because of what they say or what they do or their funny little ways. If I read a story and a character from it stays in my mind long after the story is finished, I feel it is a good story.

Trudee: What tips would you give to young writers?
Tololwa: Be patient with yourself. Even the very best writers don't like their first draft of a story. If you write something and don't think it is very good, try again.

Julie Lawson

Trudee: What kind of stories do you write?
Julie: I write a few different kinds of books. Some are stories straight from my imagination, some are folktales. *Emma and the Silk Train* is historical fiction. That means part of the story is something that really happened.

Trudee: How do you begin writing your stories?
Julie: I start with something that has caught my attention: an object, an event from history, or a catchy phrase. Then I think, "What if this happened?" and let the story flow from there.

Trudee: Do you write the whole story at once?
Julie: I write the story as I type it into my computer, making changes as I go along. When I've written the whole story, I print it out and read it over. I mark on the paper the changes I want to make. Sometimes there are lots. I type the changes into my computer, then print it out again and make more changes. For some stories I do this more than twenty times before I'm happy with it.

Trudee: What makes a good story?

Julie: I think a good story needs to touch readers. It needs to make them feel happy or sad or surprised or some other emotion. Good stories often have characters that are like us or like someone we know. That helps us understand how those characters feel and makes us care what happens to them.

Trudee: What tips would you give to young writers?

Julie: Read a lot and write a lot, even if you just scribble down some ideas. Try writing different kinds of stories, but don't be afraid to write about your own experiences and feelings. What might seem ordinary to you may be a new way of looking at something for someone else. Nobody views the world exactly the same way you do.

AFTER YOU READ

Make a list

Write three things you learned in the interviews that you can use the next time you write a story.

Emma and the Silk Train

Written by Julie Lawson
Illustrated by Paul Mombourquette

READING TIP

Use clues to figure out new words

Authors often try to explain difficult words by giving clues, such as a definition or a picture. As you read, note what clues this author gives to help you figure out new words.

"SILKER'S COMING!"

Emma ran to join her brother Charlie, drawn by the wail of the whistle, the billowing smoke, and the rhythm of wheels rolling over the rails.

"Not so close!" Mama shouted from the station window.

Charlie grabbed Emma's hand and pulled her back.

Emma didn't mind. She was still close enough to feel the ground tremble as the silk train thundered past.

Emma's pa ran the station, so she knew all the trains. The only ones she cared about were the silkers—because hidden inside was a precious cargo of silk.

Pa said the silk came over the ocean all the way from China. It was so valuable silk trains rushed it across the country to New York, stopping only long enough to change crews and hook up a fresh engine with a full head of steam. Regular trains had to wait while the silkers sped through. Once, even a royal train was moved aside for a silker.

When Emma was five, Mama had fashioned a silk blouse for herself. Emma loved how it shimmered. There was enough silk left over for a hair ribbon for Emma and two squares for her patchwork quilt. But from that moment on, Emma longed for a silk blouse of her own.

One day, Emma came home from school to find the station in an uproar.

"There's been an accident," Pa explained. "A silker's derailed. Five cars are in the river. One broke open, and bales of silk are floating downstream."

"And there's a reward!" Charlie rubbed his hands gleefully. "The railroad's paying five dollars for every bale fished out of the river!"

Emma's mind reeled. Maybe she'd find some, enough for another hair ribbon—or even a blouse, like Mama's.

The next morning, the whole town was fishing for silk.

By the end of the day, everyone had caught something.

A few people caught bales of raw silk.

Charlie caught a salmon.

Pa caught his fly-fishing hat, the one the wind had blown away the month before.

Mama caught a cold.

And Emma caught silk-fishing fever.

Long after everyone else had stopped, Emma kept fishing.

Sometimes she fished from shore.

All she caught was a gumboot.

Sometimes she fished from the wharf.

All she caught was a rusty kettle.

Sometimes she fished from the rowboat.

All she caught was disappointment.

"No more boat rides," Charlie decided one day. "Sorry, Emma, but it's been two weeks since the last silk bale was found."

But Emma didn't give up easily.

She searched the riverbank, in places where bales might be trapped by roots or partly buried in sand.

Still she found nothing.

One afternoon, Emma's search took her farther than she was allowed to go. She was rounding the bend, promising herself she would head straight back, when she saw a splash of colour a little ways from shore. The current caught the colour and unfolded it into one long rippling stream. It looked red, until the sunlight touched it. Then it shimmered gold.

"Silk!" Emma cried. Enough for a blouse like Mama's—or even a dress! Quickly, she pulled off her shoes and stockings and hitched up her skirt. Bracing herself against the cold, she waded into the river.

The water licked at the hem of her skirt and swirled around her knees.

Just a few more steps—

Emma reached out and grabbed her prize.

Triumphant, Emma turned to go back. But at that moment, the current tugged on the silk. Determined to hold on, Emma lost her balance. She gasped in panic as the river swept her off her feet.

Emma clutched the silk in her hand. She wouldn't let go. Not now! Gritting her teeth, she swam hard to reach the riverbank.

But she was no match for the current as it carried her farther and farther downstream.

Up ahead, Emma spotted a small island. Desperately, she fought the current as it threatened to pull her past.

She tried to touch bottom. Once, twice—

On the third try, her toes grazed against something. Then her foot hit the muddy bottom.

She staggered to shore and collapsed in the sand. She had made it. And she still had her silk.

But as Emma looked at the fast-flowing water between her and the distant riverbank, she began to feel uneasy. How would she get off the island?

Wet and cold, Emma huddled against a log.

She scanned the riverbank, hoping to see someone, straining to hear a voice.

Silence. The bank was deserted.

The sun crept lower in the sky. Long shadows played tricks, making bushes and branches look like people waving from shore and walking along the tracks.

Tracks! The thought of them gave Emma an idea.

Standing on the log, she tied her silk so it flowed like a banner between two trees.

Then she waited.

Shadows grew longer. The silk snapped in the rising wind.

Emma rubbed her arms and stamped her feet to keep warm.

In the distance she heard a low, shaky rumble that swelled to a locomotive roar. A train burst around the curve. A silker!

Emma jumped up and down, waving frantically. "Help!" she shouted. "It's me, Emma! STOP!"

But the train thundered past, vanishing in a cloud of flying cinders.

Emma swallowed hard. Silkers never stopped. Not for regulars, not for royalty, not for her.

The train's wailing whistle faded away, lost in the rush of the river, the sweep of the wind.

Emma waited. The sky turned black. One star appeared.

A westbound freight came into sight. Emma leaped to her feet and waved, but the train rumbled past.

A sob caught in her throat. What if no one finds me? she thought fearfully. What if I'm here all night, all alone?

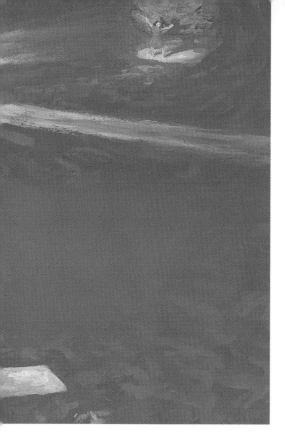

She shuddered.

Then she heard it. Faintly at first, but growing steadily stronger. Voices calling. "EM-MA! EM-MA!"

Light flickered over the water.

"Mama!" she cried. "Pa! I'm here!"

Behind her, the silk caught the light and shone.

"Emma! Are you all right?" Mama hurried out of the rowboat and swept Emma into her arms. "We were so worried!"

"Oh, Mama!" Emma burst into tears. "I was afraid you'd never find me."

Mama wrapped Emma snugly in a blanket and wiped away her tears. "Thank goodness the crew on the silker spotted that banner you made. As soon as the train reached the station, the fireman swung down from the steps—"

"The silker *stopped*?" Emma was amazed.

Mama chuckled. "Not completely. Just slowed down enough for the fireman to hand your pa the message."

They were getting into the boat when Emma looked over her shoulder. "Where's my silk?" she cried out in alarm.

"Right here," Charlie said, placing it in her
outstretched hands. "Boy, Emma. This is some catch."

As Charlie rowed to shore, Mama turned to Emma
and scolded gently. "You got a little carried away, fishing
for silk. You know you're not to go past the bend."

Emma nodded. "I'm sorry, Mama." She snuggled
closer as Mama stroked her hair. "Will it be all right?"
she asked.

Mama gave her a hug. "Now that you're safe and
sound? Of course."

"I meant—"

"And the silk will be grand, you'll see."

Emma's birthday came three weeks later.

Charlie eyed the cake hungrily. "Hurry up, Emma. Make a wish."

"Listen!" she whispered. "Silker's coming!"

A circle of light burst through the darkness. The whistle wailed as the train roared past the station.

Emma smiled. She didn't need to make a wish. Her new silk dress rustled as she leaned forward to blow out the candles.

AFTER YOU READ

Make a list of new words

Choose five new words you learned in the story. Beside each word, write what the word means. What clues helped you figure out the word?

Good Books, Good Times!

In this unit, you learned that stories have characters and there is usually a problem that needs to be solved. Now it is your turn to write a story.

⟶ Before You Begin

Think about your writing. Ask:

- What kind of story will I write: a humorous story, a family story, a folktale, or an adventure story?
- What will my story be about?
- Who will be in my story?
- Where will my story take place?
- Who will read my story?

Story Ideas

Sometimes good ideas for stories pop into your head. Write your ideas in a notebook or input them on a computer. You never know when you might use them.

A story map can help you think about what your story needs.

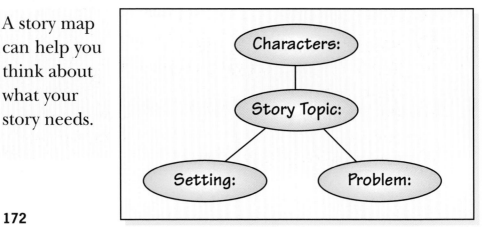

Characters:

Story Topic:

Setting:

Problem:

Your First Draft

1 Write the first paragraph.
- Write down all of your ideas.
- Don't worry about how words are spelled or if your ideas are in the right order.
- Tell your reader who's in the story and where the story is going to take place.

2 Add events to your story.
- Tell more about your characters and the problems they face.
- Use describing words and action words to make the reader feel, hear, and see what is happening.

3 Write the end of your story.
- Tell how the characters solved their problems.
- Put a surprise into your ending.
- Conclude your story.

Character
Good stories have one or more interesting characters.

Remember, good stories have a beginning that "hooks" readers and makes them want to read on.

Setting
The time and place where a story takes place is called the *setting*.

Plot
The events in a story are called the *plot*.

▶ Revise and Edit

Read your first draft carefully, as if you were reading it for the first time.

- Look for places where you can add interesting details.
- Ask yourself if it makes sense.
- Look for places where you might want to add sentences or cut sentences.
- Look for places where you might want to change the order of words or sentences.
- Check that you have used a variety of sentences.

Ask a Friend

Have a friend or classmate read your story and give their ideas about how it could be even better.

Here is part of Kailee's final story.

Once there was a dog. He lived with a girl named Lindsay, his name was Max. One day Lindsay and Max went for a walk in the mountains. There was a cat and Max started chasing it. Max got lost. He was really far away from Lindsay. He was really scared. He tried chasing a cat but he was still scared. He was hungry so he went to find a garbage can. He found one and ate from it. He was still really really hungry and his stomach was growling but there was no food left. He tried to find his way home but he got even more lost.

Publish It

You can share your story in many different ways.

- Read it aloud to your class.
- Send it to a magazine that publishes stories by kids.
- Make a class book of stories and put it in the school library for other students to read.

Think About Your Learning

- Did your story hook the reader?
- Did you create an interesting problem for your character?
- Did you use describing words and action words?
- Did you use a variety of sentences?
- Did your story have a good ending?
- Did you present your story neatly?

What did I learn?

ACKNOWLEDGMENTS

Permission to reprint copyrighted material is gratefully acknowledged. Every effort has been made to trace ownership of all copyrighted material and to secure permission from copyright holders. In the event of any question arising as to the use of any material, we will be pleased to make the necessary corrections in future printings.

Photographs

Pp. 39-51 Dave Starrett; pp. 64-65 © Corel Corporation; p. 67 (upper left, bottom) Doug Crawford, (upper right) © Corel Corporation; p. 68 Doug Crawford; p. 69 (upper left, lower right) copyright © 1998 PhotoDisc, Inc.; (upper right, lower left) © Corel Corporation; p. 71 copyright © 1998 PhotoDisc, Inc.; p. 72 (top) © Corel Corporation, (bottom) Dave Starrett; p. 73 copyright © 1998 PhotoDisc, Inc., (inset) Dave Starrett; pp. 74, 75 Dave Starrett; p. 77 copyright © 1998 PhotoDisc, Inc.; p. 80 © Corel Corporation; p. 81 copyright © 1998 PhotoDisc, Inc.; pp. 95-101 Ulli Steltzer; pp. 103-107 Dave Starrett; p. 110 Barb Eklund; p. 155 courtesy Kids Can Press; p. 156 courtesy Tololwa Mollel/University of Alberta Photo Services; p. 158 Kristin Ross

Illustrations

Cover: Allan Moon; pp. 6-7 Steve Attoe; pp. 8-11 Jenny Campbell; pp. 13-21 Janell Cannon; pp. 23-29 Rhian Brynjolson; pp. 30-37 Ted Rand; pp. 52-59 Todd L. W. Doney; pp. 60-63 Tina Holdcroft; pp. 64-65 Dave MacKay; pp. 78-79 Pat Cupples; pp. 82-89 Pat Cupples; pp. 90-93 Kim LaFave; pp. 108-111 Tina Holdcroft; pp. 112-113 Laszlo Gal; pp. 114-115 Scot Ritchie; pp. 116-117 Norman Eyolfson; pp. 118-129 Don Kilby; pp. 131-137 Cornelius Van Wright and Ying-Hwa Hu; pp. 138-141 Blanche Sims; pp. 142-145 David Beyer; pp. 146-153 Joe Weissmann; pp. 161-171 Paul Mombourquette; pp. 172-175 Tina Holdcroft

Text

"Mango Morning" by Robert Priest from DAY SONGS, NIGHT SONGS. Text copyright © 1993 by Robert Priest. Illustrations copyright © 1993 by Keith Lee. A Groundwood Book/Douglas & McIntyre. STELLALUNA, copyright © 1993 by Janell Cannon, reprinted by permission of Harcourt Brace & Company. THE YESTERDAY STONE by Peter Eyvindson. Winnipeg: Pemmican Publications Inc. 1992. Reprinted by permission. "My Buddy" from MY BUDDY. Text by Audrey Osofsky, illustrated by Ted Rand. Text © 1992 by Audrey Osofsky. Illustrations © 1992 by Ted Rand. Reprinted by permission of Henry Holt & Co. Inc.; Text and illustrations from RED BIRD by Barbara Mitchell. Illustrated by Todd L. W. Doney. Text copyright © 1996 by Barbara Mitchell. Illustrations copyright © 1996 by Todd L. W. Doney. By permission of Lothrop, Lee & Shepard Books, a division of William Morrow & Company, Inc. "The Eiffel Tower" and "Skyscrapers" from TOWERS AND TUNNELS by Etta Kaner and illustrated by Pat Cupples used by permission of Kids Can Press Ltd., Toronto. Text copyright © 1995 by Etta Kaner. Illustrations copyright © 1995 by Pat Cupples. "High Flyers" from HIGH FLYER: DESIGNING PAPER AIRPLANES FOR DISTANCE by Bob Bonnet & Dan Keen. Copyright © 1997 by Bob Bonnet and Dan Keen. Used by permission of Sterling Publishing Company, Inc. BUILDING AN IGLOO copyright © 1981 by Ulli Steltzer. A Groundwood Book/Douglas & McIntyre. "Good Books, Good Times" by Lee Bennett Hopkins. Copyright © 1985 by Lee Bennett Hopkins. Reprinted by permission of Curtis Brown, Ltd. "The Reason I Like Chocolate" by Nikki Giovanni. William Morrow & Sons.; "Hold On, McGinty!" from HOLD ON, McGINTY! © 1997 Nancy Hartry (text) and © 1997 Don Kilby (art). Reproduced with the permission of Doubleday Canada Limited. SAM AND THE LUCKY MONEY by Karen Chin. Used by permission of Lee & Low Books Inc., New York; "A Lion in the Meadow" by Margaret Mahy. Copyright © 1969, 1986 by Margaret Mahy. Used by permission of Orion Publishing Group Ltd. TWO PAIRS OF SHOES by Esther Sanderson. Winnipeg: Pemmican Publications Inc. 1990. Reprinted by permission. EMMA AND THE SILK TRAIN by Julie Lawson, illustrated by Paul Mombourquette, used by permission of Kids Can Press Ltd., Toronto. Text copyright © 1997 by Julie Lawson. Illustrations copyright © 1997 by Paul Mombourquette